CU00787845

Table of Contents

Does God Lie?

Faith then Elect   or   Elect then Faith

by
Melvin R. Nelson

xulon
PRESS

To my wife, Jean,

our three children: Carol, Bryan and Mark

to their spouses: Kent, Lisa, and Ayuna

and to the grandchildren who follow in our footsteps

and above all to

God Who loves us and sent His Son to be our Savior

Thanks to those who have read some of the work in this book and have encouraged me to share a different point of view on what can be a sensitive subject for many who study the Word of God.

Preface

Perhaps the most debated and fractious topic in Christian theology in recent years is whether we have the "free will" to put our faith in Christ. Or, does God predestine that some would be saved for reasons known only to Him? When we search the record there are many fine Bible scholars on both sides of the question. Nearly all are certain that they hold the last edge on truth. Still, there is no agreement as to what the Scriptures teach.

The root of the problem goes back to Augustine in the late 400's. Over the years he has had great influence on Christian thought. Late in life he claimed that God chose some people to believe in Christ, we have no free will to do so. Further he held that we do not know why God chose us. God does so only out of His mercy and grace. God places no condition on us; He simply gives faith in Christ to those He chose.

The logic of Augustine led to the Calvin/Arminian rift in theology. The dispute has battered the Church off and on since the 16th century. Many scars have left their mark on those that have been through the heat of friction on this matter. Not a few have been shaken in how they view God since the reasoning of both sides, if one follows their logic to the end, creates problems for how we see God. One side flirts with fatalism and the other side leads to doubt about our destiny.

This book shows another way to interpret the Scriptures on these issues. The option proposed here will challenge widely accepted views on God's elect, those He chooses. We have failed to look through the lens of the Old Testament to guide how we see the elect. Not to do so may cause problems in how we view God and His plan of the cross.

The option explained here, if Bible scholars confirm fidelity to the Word, may deal a death blow to fatalism on the one hand and insecurity about our faith in Christ on the other. The author's reasoning from the Word strengthens how we see God's faithfulness to His chosen people.

All that have looked into this subject know that the question about free will in saving faith is complex. This book presents an alternative to prior thought in this area. Scholars from both sides will need to weigh the view here against the Scriptures. But we all know that God does not lie. We just may not understand what He has said at times.

Chapter One

Free Will and Salvation

The subtitle of this book suggests a puzzle, if not a mystery; do we start first with chicken or first with egg? On the surface this may seem a small matter, one hardly worth the effort to examine or spend the time to study. Yet the problem framed a second way is: "Does God give us the faith for salvation?" Or "Do we have the free will to place our faith in Christ? As some ask, "Do we pick God or does God pick us?"

God's Word never wavers in its message; not one person would be saved unless God provided a way. He was not obliged to offer the gift of salvation to anyone. He did so by majestic and sovereign design and that at an infinite price. He sent His Son into this world to pay the penalty for our sin, to die in our place so that He could declare us righteous and give us life in Christ. In this God showed forth His love, mercy, and grace; and

He took great pleasure in the doing of His perfectly laid out plan. And the Word clearly states that those in Christ are there by God's doing (1 Cor 1:30).

Therefore the matter of free will is complex; and Bible scholars have debated the issue for centuries. As we look into this problem we tread on Holy ground. We dare not trifle with what God has ordained to happen, lest we fail to give glory to Him for Who He is and what He does. We must also take care not to lead others down the wrong path of doctrine.

How we view and proclaim the Gospel, the good news about Christ, is at stake. What looks like certainty in our minds may in the end lead to a slippery slope and damage the message of God's love in sending His Son to a sin ravaged people. How we present God to a lost world is critical. Who we say He is, and what we say He has done, can have grave consequences for all that might consider God's wondrous gift.

This indeed is a serious and demanding venture; we will direct our efforts to try to understand the very Words of God as He spoke through His servants of old. Heaven forbid that we speak other than, or more than what He has said; for we weigh vital life and death truths in the balance.

So with cautious trepidation I ask what needs to be asked. "Does God promise to choose those who have faith in Christ for salvation?" Or "Does God choose people and then give those people faith in Christ as well as salvation?"

These are sobering questions because of where the answers might lead. But we must face the options of this debate head on; to dodge the implications serves the good of no one. On the one hand we might be mere pawns in the hands of God as He works out His perfect will through us and brings glory to Christ; then we can thank Him that He has chosen us for His side. Or, on the other hand God may say we have a measure of choice, such that we can choose to believe, or not so choose.

There are a few peripheral concerns to this debate. But if we can resolve the heart of the matter, then most of the less important claims will fade from lack of support. Or they will rise from a credible base.

I will not address the minor areas in this book. Rather I will try to deal with what, to me, has become the pivotal axis throughout the Scriptures: Who are "God's elect"? Then in the final two chapters we will look at a few of the implications for the view taught here.

The key questions that drive this study are:

1. Is God's grace so irresistible that people have no choice but to accept and believe in Christ?

2. Is humanity so depraved that no one can believe in Christ without God giving us the faith to do so?

3. Does God appoint us to eternal life before we believe?

4. Is the offer of salvation genuine to all that hear?

History of the Debate

The question on whether we have the free will to believe in Christ goes back hundreds of years. While many eminent scholars of the Word are quite assured that they know what the Scriptures teach, there is no consensus. When we search the record we find that there are those on both sides of the debate. And where two sides exist, both which claim to be right on such vital things, there will be confusion for those who look on. And as sad as it may be, we know that strife about such matters has at times left deep scars on those who have been through the heat of conflict about this question.

Augustine was the first to open the door to this polemic in the early 400's. He taught that God picks people to be saved by His sovereign will alone. God gives people faith in Christ; we do not choose to believe of our own free volition.

The dispute remained high profile until the Synod of Orange in 529. Then the church rejected some of what he taught. Rather that synod reached the verdict that we cannot come to faith in Christ unless God gives "prevenient" grace to do so; but the meaning of such grace was never made clear. In spite of their vagueness of notion and a lack of support from the Word they still ruled at the time that with this grace we can choose to believe in Christ; without such grace we cannot.

Then the stir of friction fell nearly silent for many years. But the question revived with the full force of a church-wide brawl during the days of the Reformers. Church leaders of that day chose up sides and the dispute hit its peak in the 16th and 17th centuries when advocates of Arminius' thought (pro free will) clashed head to head with those of Calvin (no free will).

Out of that Word smithing fracas came the Synod of Dort in 1619. The Dort Council proposed five fundamental pillars for the Calvin point of view, now known by the acrostic T-U-L-I-P. In sequential order these are the Total Depravity of Man, Unconditional Election, Limited Atonement, Irresistible Grace, and Perseverance of the Saints.

Ever since that day Bible scholars have gone back and forth on one or more of these five basics. The spat of division has knocked the Church around, off and on, for close to four hundred years. While most leaders of Christendom have meant well the debate has not been pretty at times.

Out of the parting of the ways a number of church groupings have carved their niche; though not solely based on these issues. In the main, the Reformed and Presbyterian hold to a strict Calvin point of view. To them God gives us faith in Christ, we do not choose Christ of our own free will. In fact they allege there is no such thing as free will to believe.

Most traditional Baptist and kindred churches tend to be on the moderate side of God's sovereign rule and free will. They, like the Calvinists, hold that once we are saved we will always be saved. But these moderates claim that we must first choose to put our faith in Christ, and we do so of our own free will.

Most of the charismatic and those that lean toward an emphasis on obedience or works to remain saved hold to unfettered free will. The last church grouping will often teach that a person can lose their salvation. We are not secure in Christ unless we maintain our faith in Him.

Then there are single or subsets of churches that switch sides from time to time. This may depend on the leaders of a church, and what they teach for doctrine. Some teachers can be quite convincing and most people do not realize there is a marked contrast between the two views.

A few churches stay out of the entire imbroglio; as they insist on no single point of view. They do not make these issues a case for orthodoxy. Perhaps they have done so out of wisdom or from fear of conflict, but more likely due to a lack of study in doctrine. While free from what at times can divide, some of these churches may be weak on other basics, those that require sound teaching in the Word.

Brief Review of the Five Calvin Pillars

In order to launch our study from common ground I will spell out each of the five Calvin basics as seen from both sides of the fence on free will. I do not intend a sweeping search of Scripture or the examination of all the fine details here; that goes far beyond where we need to be at this moment in our quest.

Only a brief review of the basics is required to help us walk on the same path of study. But keep in mind that there are a variety of nuances to both sides on all five points. What I write here are just the typical convictions that most embrace from each camp.

Total Depravity of Man

Calvin scholars who claim that we have no "free will" to choose Christ say that all mankind is under spiritual death since the Fall of Adam. To them this means that we are not able to respond to God in any shape or form. All that we can do is sin; we are corrupt in our total being. No one tries to understand God; no one will ever seek God. Left on our own we have no capacity or will to believe. God must always take the first step toward us, and to them this includes choosing us and giving us faith in Christ. They claim Romans 3:10-18 as a prime source of support for this teaching.

Most students of the Word from the camp that holds to "free will" also teach that God seeks the lost and without His seeking no one would come to Christ. *"For the Son of Man has come to seek and to save that which was lost"* (Lk 19:10). *"He first loved us"* (1 Jn 4:19). Nevertheless they claim that people still must respond to the God Who seeks. While all people are spiritually dead, we still have the free will to come to Christ when God seeks us through His messengers and through His Word. We are not so dead that we cannot believe. God gives us the new birth when we choose to trust in His Son.

Some "free will" scholars claim too that the Word tells us that the lost can seek God. They use verses such as Isaiah 55:6; Deuteronomy 4:29; Jeremiah 29:12-13; Amos 5:4-6; Acts 17:26-27; and Hebrews 11:6 to bolster their view. Such scholars often say that the verb for "seek" in Romans 3:11 is a diligent or steady type of seeking that comes after salvation.

Those of a strict Calvin bent say in reply that those who seek in any manner do so by God's will. They are His elect; God has chosen them. They would not be saved unless God acted to cause them to seek.

Unconditional Election

Calvin patrons say that God has His chosen people, called the elect. Since He chose them in Christ before He created the world there are no conditions placed on them to be given salvation, not even faith. God gives both faith and salvation to those He chose. If you happen to be one of the elect God will do all the work to reach you and to work within you to save you. On the other hand if you are not one of His elect you will not be saved. Calvinists see this view as the only one that is all of God's grace. Their texts for such claims are Ephesians 1:3-11; Romans 8:29-30, 9:6-23; and 1 Corinthians 1:27-29, among others.

Those who teach that man has "free will" say that we must choose to put our faith in Christ. Those who have this faith in Christ are the elect, and God gives them the new birth. Some go on to say that God has no condition for giving His gift of salvation to us. But to receive the gift there is one condition, we must have faith in Christ (Geisler, 2001). The Biblical source for this teaching is found throughout the Word and is seen in the oft repeated prompting, counsel, and warning to put our faith in Christ. They claim that God knew those that would put their faith in Christ before the world began but He does not cause them to do so.

Limited Atonement

Those who firmly hold fast to the Calvin basics say that Christ died only for those whom God chose, His elect. They use texts that say that Christ died for "many" (Mt 1:21, 20:28, 26:28; Heb 9:28) rather than for "all". And they identify the "many" as the sheep that belong to Christ before they believe in Him (Jn 10:15, 26-28).

When they read the text of John 3:16 which says, *"God so loved the world,"* they claim that the verse actually refers to all the Gentiles and Jews from around the world who make up His elect. Christ did not die for those whom God did not choose, because if He did, then all would be saved. But, the Scriptures clearly teach that not all will be saved (Mt 25:41; 2 Thes 1:8-9).

In contrast those that hold to human free will say that Christ died for the entire world. Verses such as John 3:16 should be read in their plain sense. They hold that while Christ died for all (Jn 1:29; 4:42; 2 Cor 5:19; 1 Jn 2:2, 4:14), only those who receive what He did by faith will benefit from what He did on the cross.

There are many Bible scholars that reject "limited atonement." Yet they still claim to hold to the other four Calvin pillars. In their study they find that the textual base for this doctrine is weak. Hence they call themselves four-point Calvinists, just as they say Calvin himself was. When they read his works they find that he did not teach this view; only those who followed in his path did so (Geisler, 2001).

While some scholars are indeed four pointers, they are not as strict in how they explain the other four points. Highly strict guardians of Calvin thought would say in turn that what this group teaches does not comport with the Word of God; they fudge with the truth.

Irresistible Grace

The hard line Calvin position states that if God chooses us to be saved we cannot and will not resist. Grace conquers all. God will work within us to help us want to be saved, and He will save us. He will use all means to give us belief in Christ even to the point of forcing the unwilling. Those that teach this say that God works His will through His grace for those He chose. No one can resist His will. They claim that if there is any condition on our part, such as belief, then salvation is not of true grace. Their

Scriptural base for this view includes Luke 14:23, John 6:44, and Romans 9:15-22, among others.

In contrast those that adhere to a measure of "free will" teach that people can resist God's grace and not put their faith in Christ. We must choose to believe. The Bible verses they use to support their claims include 1 Timothy 2:4 and 2 Peter 3:9. These Scriptures clearly say that God desires all to be saved. If He desires all to be saved then the only reason that people are not saved is that they resist the Holy Spirit (Acts 7:51) or God's will (Lk 7:30); most do not and will not believe in Christ.

Perseverance of the Saints

Calvin scholars say that the saved can never lose their salvation; once a child of God we will always be a child of God. We are secure in Christ for all the future, even when we sin. What God starts He will see through to the end; all those who once believe in Christ arrive in heaven. God completes His will in the life of those who are His. There is nothing that can keep the elect from the love of God in Christ. Some of the texts for this view are John 6:39-40, 10:27-28; Romans 8:29-30, 8:37-39; and 2 Timothy 1:12.

Some, but not all, that hold to strict "free will" say that we can lose our salvation through lack of, or giving up our belief. Some go so far as to say that habitual sin can cause one to fall out of grace. A few of their Scriptures are 1 Corinthians 9:27, Galatians 5:4, and Hebrews 6:4-6, 10:26-29.

There are those on the moderate "free will" side who think that staunch Calvin sponsors go much too far on the first four of the five basics, but agree with them on this last point. Those not so strict in their Calvin bent claim that once we are part of the elect through faith in Christ, we belong to Him forever. We cannot lose our salvation. They agree that God works out His will in the life of those who believe in Christ and they will be

His for all the future. Most that claim this use the same texts as those who are narrower in their Calvin creed.

The Debate in Recent Years

As C. Hansen wrote of late in <u>Christianity Today</u> (2006) the debate over "free will" and saving faith has been known to flare to a flash point in some Christian groups. A few churches have been known to split when the heat of who's right and who's wrong rends the Body, scattering the flock to the four winds. On the surface the differences should not cause that much conflict. But there are always a few that will fight tooth and nail as they insist that the way they read God's Word is the one and only right way.

People in the pew who are taught only one side of the question on free will often don't know the fret. They leave the tough stuff for the theologians. Most don't even know that there is more than one way to look at the Scriptures in this arena. They search no further than what they hear from those they trust; they avoid or neglect devoted study to see if what is taught from the pulpit fits with the balance of God's Word. From their point of view the pastor has had the training in theology; and as a rule the pastor is right. For the most part this is a fairly good assumption to make in most evangelical churches, but not always.

Others of faith start to question and search, as is common when they first hear or read about a different way to understand some of the texts. Those that study the question find that there are solid, loving, and well-taught Christians who shine the light on the Word in a way that they had not heard before. They become amazed that the Scriptures can be so alive and profound when seen from a different point of view. In fact some find that these other Christians know the Word far better than they do. Then the appealing new look begins to make reasonable sense to them. Those in the hunt for more depth in their walk with the

Lord are often the most persuaded; they want to know God more and they want to be skilled in His Word.

With what looks like keen new insights into the Scriptures some will shift sides. A few tend to become overzealous as they try to convince others of their newly found grasp of what they see as Word based doctrine. A few become angry and fault their former teachers for misleading them. Or they charge that those who taught them lacked a competent knowledge of the Word, or they didn't know doctrine very well; or they were tainted by error.

Others who have a strong bias in favor of what they had been taught in the past may look at a new interpretation of the Word with distrust. They ask, "How could anyone think that way?" To them the new point of view, which is not new at all, must be the next thing to heresy. The certain and dogmatic that object to all views, distinct from their own, can be quick to offend and provoke. They may rise up to fight for what they have been taught before, or what they have held for a long period of time.

None of us are immune from rigid views when it comes to what we perceive as the basics of doctrine. But we need to be more than cautious in our certainty when there are faithful and learned Christians who see things from a different point of view. Not everyone can be right. And we won't know the final answers on many questions until we get to heaven. Then none of us will care, as all the saved will come to know and celebrate the same things. Our eyes will be opened and we will praise and worship God for Who He is and what He has done.

We also need to bear in mind that there are mysteries in the Word that we cannot fathom with our weak human minds. The wisdom of God goes infinitely beyond the wisdom of Man. We must say, along with Paul that now we only know in part; we see through a glass darkly (1 Cor 13:12). Still, all true Christians know and accept that God works out His will; there is nothing too hard for God (Gn 18:14; Jer 32:27; Lk 1:37).

Words will never fully capture the essence of Who God is, what He does, and how He does it. Our minds cannot begin to fathom the idea of complete perfection in all things. We are much too prone to confine Him to a box and say that He can and will do things only in the way we think that He does them.

Perhaps at times we may be right, but does that mean we should part the church body over insights gained by labor in the Word, and perhaps enlightenment, but which others may not see? May it never be! Does that show love for the brethren? And God's Word gives clear warning to the one that would divide the body of Christ (Titus 2:10-11). Too many churches have split over these issues, and good friends in the Lord become suspect.

Even so we should always strive to be as faithful as we can be to the texts of God's sacred Word. All good students of the Bible will try to do just that. We must take care to recognize and refute flawed hermeneutics. We dare not champion teaching that promotes for dogma what is but possible. And more, where the Word is silent we should not speak in its place. We must have enough integrity at such times to own up to the fact that we do not know what God has said. An opinion is no substitute for His Truth.

As humbled as we may be, we may not even realize at times that we have fallen into a pitfall of error. We are too often charmed by what we think, certain that we see the Word the correct way. How could we make a mistake? After all, we have the Holy Spirit to guide us.

In the debate set forth in this book not everyone can be right. There is a right way and a number of wrong ways to look at the Scriptures on the question of free will in salvation. For some reason God has not seen a need to make clear what He has said.

Either that or some of us do not want to accept the truth. Certainly few of us want to think that our future was cast in stone before we were born. And we don't want to think that God has not chosen a family relative, while He did choose us. And we want to think we are secure in the faith regardless of what we might do.

Yet all of us that belong to Christ, no matter which side of the debate we are on, know that we do not, and will never, deserve what God has done for us in Christ. Without God's mercy and grace we would never be saved, we would never live our life in Christ, and we would never see heaven.

Needless to say not one person that knows the Word well comes to this area of study without a preferred way to see things. We have our doctrines that we hold to, or a traditional view that has been good enough for us. We have all had teachers who taught us well and some poorly.

Then some of us go to the Word in our personal search and cannot make sense of what has been written. First we end up on one side, and then we study more and we end up on the other side. Then we burrow deeper yet, and we go back to where we started.

If the Word is not clear then the subject must not be all that important. That is what I have been taught over the years. And so as a rule I stay out of the fray and let others wrestle with the Word in this area of study. And for most of my life there has been little contention between those who claim differing views. We have all gotten along without pushing the buttons of those who see the Scriptures from their distinct point of view on the posed questions.

But I have observed a growing tension and foment in recent years voiced by partisans of polar camps. And I have heard the groans of those caught in the throws of some who want to make a big "to do" that their way is God's way. None of this is very

Christian-like, and the rush to insist we are right can stoke smoldering coals into a blazing fire. We don't need more dissension among the saints and in the churches.

And the inferno is roaring hot in some places such as on a few websites. Some self-absorbed Christians hurl fire and brimstone at fellow members of the body of Christ as they review each other's books and creedal stands in this area of study. To the chagrin of all that love the Lord and the Church, this takes place for the whole world to see. I do not think God is well pleased.

In contrast there have been a few excellent books in recent years on the doctrine of salvation. One that I prize is B. Demarest' (1997) "The Cross and Salvation." His approach to the subject of the "elect" and free will is very balanced. His review of the history of thought in this area is superb. In the end he moves toward the Calvin version of the elect, and this is common for many fine scholars of the Word.

All the same, I think the Scriptures differ from some of what he concludes. But his book does not cover the view to be presented here. I doubt that he is aware that there is yet another way to interpret God's Word on this matter; one that I have not found in print.

A few other books have chafed raw nerves as heavy weights for the Calvin and free will camps (e.g. D. Hunt & J. White, 2004) contest each other's views. While dialogue is worthy and should be pursued, many that read such books sense the friction. And such friction can lead to schisms that threaten to divide the body of Christ in local assemblies. Over the years the debate between rival sides has led to more rancor than détente. And there doesn't seem to be any end for those who insist that their way is God's way.

Most theologians enter the dispute to do no more than expound and fine tune viewpoints that date back hundreds of years. And there are sagacious scholars of the Word on both sides of the issue. Few have seen or proposed any new way to look at the Scriptures. All hues of the spectrum are fairly certain that they interpret the Scriptures the right way. But I'm not so sure that I have read anyone that does so on this subject.

Authors such as R. C. Sproul, in his book "Chosen by God" (1986), J. White in, "The Potter's Freedom," (2000), and "The God Who Justifies" (2001), J. Piper in, "The Justification of God" (1993, 2nd ed), and writers in T. Schreiner and B. Ware's (ed.) "Still Sovereign" (2003), all have a strong mind for God's control in all things. Saving faith is not a choice that we make. Rather God, by His grace, gives us the faith to be saved. And more, God by His sovereign will sets in motion all decisions that we will ever make. Not even a slight nod is given in the direction of a person having the free will to choose. People do what God wills them to do, no more and no less.

For the most part the debate on free will has focused on the area of salvation. But some theologians from both extremes toy with lesser known issues too; they press skewed ideas to their logical limit. To the dismay of most, the human intellect can seize on things that begin to corrupt, if not desecrate, the way God is portrayed. The problem may not be a doctrine itself but rather how far one wants to push the implications of that doctrine.

A few scholars on the fringes carry the idea of God's absolute control to a much further end. They say that God rules the lost in all their ways. People oppose and rebel against God, and they do so by God's design and purpose. To them God controls each and every single act, not just in fixing a limit or guiding how they sin, but causing them to sin. To them Satan is not one thing more than a tool in God's hands. Some teach that God went so far as to orchestrate the mutiny of Satan and then the Fall of Man in the garden. They say that the ultimate purpose for sin is to bring more glory to Christ as God will sum up all things in His Son (Eph 1:10).

Yet these same hierologists still see people as culpable and God as just for sending the sinner to Hell. This they say because God can do and does what He wants. His actions are always right simply because He wills them; and of course no one can argue with that.

But if they hold this view then they must claim that His sovereign rule pulls rank over the essence of all other aspects of His character. To these scholars we are little more than puppets under the thumb of God; freedom to choose is no more than an illusion. God selects some to be saved for reasons known only to Him, and He took great delight in doing so. They flirt with fatalism; we have naught to say about our destiny, and no one ever has, not even Adam.

Others who grapple with such issues have taken a position under a different flag. They claim that God is sovereign but He acts through knowing all things; He is omniscient. God knows the choices that people will make and He knows those people who will accept and put their faith in Christ. Man is free to choose and does so in the matter of salvation.

To most advocates, God does influence us to choose to come to Christ. The Holy Spirit is always active, but God does not coerce. Rather He shapes the future through the will of all people who make their own choices. We are free agents and God uses His own means and circumstances to carry out what He has in mind. Those who lean toward the Arminius side on "free will" tend to reason this way.

From this camp would be an author such as Robert Picirilli who wrote "Grace, Faith, and Free Will" (2002). He seems to do a fine job of defending the original thoughts on 'free will' that came from Arminius. To him we have the freedom to choose to believe in Christ.

Robert Shank took a second approach in his book, "Elect in the Son" (1989). He seems to agree with Karl Barth's view as explained in his "Church Dogmatics", Volume II, Part 2 (translated into English 1967, Bromiley, G. W. & Torrence, T. F., ed.). They both defend "free will" from a corporate point of view; Christ is the chosen One, and hence those who believe Christ are in the chosen One of God. But to get into Christ we must decide of our free will to put our faith in Him.

While I value the work and study of these last men, and they are quite skilled in the Word, I still have not found any of their views to be that persuasive. The texts used by those who adhere to Calvin precepts are much too potent in what they say. Yet there may be a better way to read these Scriptures; and we will soon pursue that course.

In the past two decades some theologians have gone to a position under a third flag; and they tread on very thin and treacherous ice. Clark Pinnock et al with the book on the "Openness of God" (1994) is just such a case. He and a few others seem to elevate the free will of man to be somewhat above God's rule. From their perspective God does not know all things, since He does not control all things. He is aware of some of the future, but not everything. In fact God can be surprised. To them, when God is surprised He can change His mind and go in a new direction. Such claims raise serious doubts about how they view God; He doesn't seem to be the One we read about in the Bible. Their God is not omniscient.

The last position is perhaps just a human inspired rebuff to the ultra determinism of the far reaches of Calvin thought. But both the last view and that of tightly held Calvinism seem to shade, if not distort certain axioms of Scripture. That this is so for Open Theism is clear to most orthodox sages of the Word. But the twists of the far Calvin side are not so easy to sort out. We need to look at the Scriptures with utmost care to discern what is going on.

In rebuttal to the far extremes of Calvin and "free will" camps Norman Geisler wrote "Chosen But Free" (2001, 2nd ed.). He claims a middle of the road view that concurs with some of the tenets of Calvin creed, but he rejects others. He says that the Word teaches the sovereign rule of God while still giving Man a voice. To this sapient scholar, God's will is merely co-extensive with what we freely decide. In other words God works His will through our free choice. God never coerces the unwilling. God places no condition on us for salvation, it is a gift; but for us to receive this gift of grace we have one need, faith in Christ.

To support his position Geisler surveyed what the early church fathers wrote. He found that nearly all of them saw faith as a choice. There was but one exception, Augustine in the 400's. And he too held that faith in Christ was a choice until late in life when he fought the famed doctrine battles with the Pelagians. This errant group thought that people were not fully corrupt in their sin nature; hence they taught that in their moral self-effort they could decide for Christ and also live for Him. The Pelagian view undercut the need for God's grace in all of life.

Geisler's work goes a long way towards the marriage of free will and God's sovereign rule. He would temper three of the first four points of T-U-L-I-P, reject limited atonement outright, and leave the fifth point, the perseverance of the saints, intact. He agrees that once we believe Christ we cannot lose our salvation.

Yet, strict Calvinists reject Geisler's work (White, 2000) because they read the texts in their own distinct way. Likewise I find his exegesis of the key texts used by astute Calvin scholars to be rather weak, if not fully anemic. And this goes too for others who have defended free will, including Hunt in his debate with White (D. Hunt & J. White, 2004). There may be a better and more accurate way to go.

Over the years there have been a few men of the Word who have tried to stake out a centrist position and tread a path between a strict Calvin persuasion and complete "free will." Most recent is C. Olson (2002) in his "Beyond Calvinism and Arminianism. A Mediate View." Both he and Laurence Vance in "The Other Side of Calvinism" (1999), have some keen insights into the Gospel of John which support some of the thinking yet to be explained here. But the way they read the book of Acts and the Pauline texts left much to be desired; in the end what they said came to little more than what most had said before from the "free will" camp.

Proposing a New View

The option that I will present in this book is not in print to my knowledge; though I cannot claim to have read everything in print. But I also have not found any referenced work that teaches this view. Hence, I can only assume that what I will explain has not been tested or examined by scholars who study the texts.

The option proposed here is driven by the Biblical text as written and read in the milieu of the first years of the Church age. There is a core teaching in the Word that scholars ignore from both sides of the debate on free will. This new view (which would not be new if held by those who wrote the NT) might help shed some light on the subject.

The English wording, at least in the New American Standard Bible (NASB) and the New International Version (NIV), will suffice to sort out the problem. A modicum of help from the Greek language can serve to guide us too. But those who want to pursue more in depth study of the Greek texts should do so to verify or refute what will be said here.

The new point of view that will be taught here may not change many minds, as most of us get stuck in how we read the text of the Word. Yet I think that what I write here will give all sides pause to re-evaluate as both Calvin and "free will" scholars may be partly right and partly wrong. Or, on the other hand, I may be completely wrong. But we do know and all accept that God's Word cannot be wrong. We just may not understand what He has said at times.

Avid champions of Calvin thought are sold out to what they think is God's truth. Since they are enthused and the texts seem to lean toward them, they attract many to their way of handling the texts. Most good commentaries follow suit; and except for a few key wrinkles I might agree with how they look at the texts.

To this date I have not read a counter position, from the free will camp, that levels a serious challenge to the way strict Calvin scholars read the fourth Gospel, the book of Acts, and the Pauline texts. Yet there is a major hitch in what they teach. They ignore one of the most basic axioms in all of Scripture.

Those who hold to "free will" in saving faith can be just as convinced and strident about their side. But I find their arguments somewhat vague and not nearly as persuasive when I explore what they say text by text. If what I am going to write is correct, then those who hold to a hard line on "free will" may need to modify their thinking too. I doubt that they read the texts in the right way. They ignore the same core axiom.

Let me say from the start that the focus of our efforts should always be on the text of the Word. Text should drive doctrine, not the other way around. And more, we dare not ignore or fail to appreciate the day in which a text was written. We need to read and understand the Word in the way it was written to derive the truth of any text.

Bible scholars of our day must take great care not to put the framework of their derived doctrine above the Word. With due regard to those who have gone before, past commentary may at times lead to eisegesis (reading a meaning into a text), not exegesis (reading what the text says). These things are so for all that strive toward fidelity to the Word.

No doubt most of us who take sides in the debate think we hold the high ground on truth. As fervent Christians we want to be faithful to the Word of God, and most of us who study are convinced that we at least come close. And I do not want to even suggest a laxity on the part of any honest theologian, pastor or otherwise. After all, the debate on these issues has been around for centuries. But here and there preconceived dogma can get in our way. Such dictum can lead us to mold the texts to fit our ideas rather than the other way around.

By the time you reach the last page of this book you may conclude that I have slanted the texts too. Nonetheless you will finish with a new way to look at what the Scriptures say in this arena. I expect at the bare minimum that what I write will cause many to dig deeper into the Word. Such pursuit is always good for us as long as it does not take us away from living out our faith in Christ.

Bible scholars, far more skilled than I, will likely persist in a debate on these issues for years to come. They have done so since the days of Augustine and even more so over the past five hundred years. But we might as well have one more perspective to put in the mix. Maybe one will be right. Or, on the other hand perhaps we will all be amazed at how misguided we have been when we get to heaven.

While I know the subject at hand is tough, and many have strong feelings about it, I still lean toward what I will write here. I do so only after much study and thought. But, you will need to dig through the texts of Scripture for yourself. In this you will need to weigh the exegesis spelled out here to see if it fits with the balance of God's Word.

I do not present what follows to add more confusion to the subject, nor to add fuel to any fires. Still, we need to give certain Scriptures their due weight before we forge our doctrine.

Since this is a new view, not in print to my knowledge, I am aware that I walk on hazardous turf. There will be those who disagree, and perhaps strongly. But if this proposed view holds water, then all sides of the debate have been more than a tad off base since the time of late Augustine.

So I write for your prayerful review. I would not take the time to put this on paper unless I thought there was ample defense. Yet, all should search the Word to convince themselves on these matters.

My own views are subject to change if I should find that God's Word teaches something else. And yes, through time I have changed my view on this subject, being more persuaded by the voice of Scripture than by the commentary of men. And what I will say is different than what has been said before. Hence I urge all who read this book to verify or refute what I say by a close and thorough study of the texts used.

The Debate as arranged in this book

As said earlier in this first chapter the debate in this book is arranged around the Biblical concept of God's "elect." Who are they? Second, what is the role of faith for His elect? Do we become one of the elect before or after faith? Do we have the free will to believe?

I will call those on one side of the debate "elect then faith." This side claims that God chose to give an elect group of people both faith and salvation. Most proponents say that God has full control, and man has no free will to choose to believe. People are so depraved that faith in Christ is not an option for anyone.

People belong to God without condition before they have faith in Christ. Those who stick either to an Augustinian or a resolute five point Calvin interpretation of God's Word hold that this is what the Scriptures teach.

The second side of the debate I will call "faith then elect." Adherents exhort that we are free to choose to believe in Christ. They say that God grants a common grace to all, and part of this common grace is the capacity to believe. God reveals Himself in a number of ways, but most through His creation, His Word, in Christ, and by the convicting power of the Holy Spirit. We can resist what He has revealed or we can accept Christ and put our faith in Him.

To this side, the work of salvation was done in Christ. Faith has no value or merit of itself. Faith is not a work. Rather, Christ, the object of faith has all merit. His work on the cross is a gift, but all must accept the gift through faith in Christ. No one belongs to God before they exercise this faith. Those who tilt toward Arminius claim that the Scriptures teach these precepts. I will not develop the ideas of this last point of view to the fullest; others have done so, some of whom were mentioned before.

Rather, I will give a third option that leads to a new way to read the debated texts; one that says that we are free to choose while God gives us faith in Christ, our salvation. What I will attempt to show does not fully support Arminius' thought on free will in salvation. But neither does the option add weight to the idea of God's total control. This new view, if true, will modify three of the five points under TULIP, reject one point in full, and leave one intact with no change. I call this proposed view "faith to faith."

Stick with me as we go through the Scriptures to capture the essence of this "faith to faith" approach. What I will show will be new for most students of the Word. Going to a Bible commentary will not help much, as I haven't read any that concurs in full. Therefore, I intend to go through the Scriptures with care, all the difficult texts. And we will look most intently at the proof texts that strict Calvinists hang their hat on for the first four of their five basic pillars.

I will show from the Word that the debate over the years has ignored a fundamental truth of the Scriptures. And this truth will change how we read a number of the most contested texts of the NT. In this you will find that we have the free will to believe; yet faith in Christ, our salvation, is a gift from God. The next chapters of this book will stretch and challenge your doctrine on salvation. This will be so no matter where you have stood before on the debate about free will. Theologians call this area of study by the term soteriology. We must ask, "How does God save us?"

Chapter Two

The Historical Setting:

Belief and Unbelief

While culture will never trump or change God's timeless truth, we still must read a text in the light of the day in which the authors wrote. Hence, before we take our probing search into the depths of God's Word let's take a brief but focused tour through the historical and religious era at the time of Christ. And we need to do the same for the Roman world of Paul's day. With a close look at a few things from the background of those early years of faith in Christ we may well come to the Scriptures more ready to get a grip on what some texts teach.

We should never divorce an author's words from the milieu of their generation. To do so with the Scriptures is out and out negligence; such leads to all kinds of problems for both interpretation and application. In this we are prone to stretch, narrow, or fully miss the meaning of that which God's servants have written. Then we forfeit the truth; or we will wrench it out of shape. Alas, we perhaps may not even recognize the truth, even when the light from God's Word stares us in the face.

Besides the milieu of the author's day, all good students of the Word know too that we must take the pains to sort through the written context. Themes, verb forms, the native language, who the author is, to whom they wrote, and the like, are all musts to track down. We slacken on these to the peril that we stray from the pure message of what the author meant and what God has said.

For our study on the elect we need to work our way through a short list of observations from the milieu and culture of that day. This is imperative. Such a review may help us get our minds around what the NT says about free will and saving faith.

These truths are part of the fabric woven into the lives of those who lived at the time of Christ and the first years after His ascension. Some of these known, but all too ignored facts, from that day may prompt us to take one more look at the way we read the letters of Paul, the book of Acts, and the four Gospels.

This brief survey of the given context of those years that bridge the OT to the NT may at first seem to make the exegesis of Scripture more complex than need be. Yet with some prudent thought the cadre of facts from that era may shed some light on our path. We need to think in terms of how they would have read Paul in the light of the Scriptures that they had, not in terms of reading the whole NT.

With the valid findings below in hand we may be able to read texts that before seemed awkward and hard to grasp. Some phrases and words of a few thorny texts never seem to quite add up. Now, many are clearer, at least to me. I have grown to know and value the milieu out of which the NT Scriptures came to us.

Stay with me for now. The reason for such an exercise will become more evident as we take this tour through the culture of the early years of the Church age.

The Early New Testament Era

To prepare the way for the "faith to faith" option, we need to look at eight facts of substance from that period of transition. These include the following.

1. Hebrew non-believers in Palestine.
2. Hebrew believers in Palestine.
3. The greatest OT Prophet.
4. Expectations for the Messiah.
5. OT Scriptures only (No NT).
6. Men of Israel in every city.
7. The distribution of the OT across the known world.
8. The men who wrote the books of the NT.

Hebrew Nonbelievers in Palestine

All told, the vast majority of the Hebrew people did not turn to Christ. They were the blind who were led by the blind. Most made their bed with the falsely pious leaders who did not accept Christ. Proud of their works and self-righteous ways they saw no need for a Savior.

Most were too busy, too wrapped in self, taken by position, family, wealth, or the pursuit of other aims, to give time to a carpenter. And He was from a town scorned by most. What good could come from that place (Jn 1:46)? And the coming of God's King and Prophet was not to be from Galilee (Jn 7:40-52).

The blind that led, including nearly the whole of the Sanhedrin, rejected Christ too. The known exceptions, in that ruling body of the Jews, were Nicodemus and Joseph of Arimethea.

We know that Christ was routinely in a barbed clash with the elite "clerics" of the land: most Scribes, Pharisees, and Sadducees. These cunning and devious leaders were jealous of the crowds that thronged to Christ. They were steeped in tradition and law; they held that they were the righteous ones. They kept the laws that they felt would earn them points with God. In their minds they were chosen by God; they said that Abraham was their father (Jn 8:39). They pulled few punches in their ongoing duel with the Son of God as they began to plot His death.

As Paul wrote in Romans 10:3, most of the Hebrew people led by the clerics, set about to be righteous. They refused to submit to what God wanted. They had no true faith in God; and clearly they did not love God. They did not rely on God's mercy, as they saw no need for mercy in their lives; they thought that God would honor and accept their "good works." They failed to concede that God is Holy and perfectly righteous; He cannot and will not tolerate one whiff of sin. He only accepts the righteousness that He provides for us in Christ, that which is without blemish (Heb 9:14).

The Hebrew people might have been looking for a Messiah, but not a humble servant. They expected their king to throw off the rule of Rome and bring in the longed for earthly realm of David's heir, but not the One Who would die on the cross. They saw no need for what God offered. Most were so blind and self-sufficient that they could not even see the awesome works that Christ was doing. And when they did see His works they heard the rumors fed by most of their leaders; His power came from the ruler of demons (Mt 12:24; Jn 8:48-52).

Hebrew Believers in Palestine

Then again, was the lack of belief the full story in the land of promise at the time Christ was born in the small village where David once lived? How many people in the land loved God when Christ came to this earth? Were there none, a few, more than a few, or many? Would Mary, Joseph, Zacharias, and Elizabeth be among those who held to true faith in God? Do the magi from a distant land count? Do the shepherds on the hills of Judea?

What about thirty years later? Could I persuade you to think that there were many, if not large numbers, in the land of that day who truly believed God when Christ first took the public stage? This would include most of His disciples and those who first followed Him. The key question that we need to ponder is, "Did they believe, let alone know, that Christ was the Son of God from the start?"

Most Hebrew people would have known the OT very well. They heard and read Moses every Sabbath in the synagogue; this took place in most towns across their country. They read the other prophets too; they knew what God had promised. They heard what David had taught; and they certainly claimed that they were in the lineage of Abraham.

They had by then heard and learned all that God had done for them through the past years. Few, if any, had stooped to the worship of idols after they returned to the homeland from their exile to Babylon some 500 plus years before. Most heeded all the sacrifices and feast days found in the OT. Most went to the Holy City to take part in the Passover and other feast days; they all held to their traditions. Their culture had a wealth of truth given to them by God.

Still we must admit that most people in that day skimmed over or neglected what God told them in the OT. When they did go to the Sacred Scrolls they were prone to twist or distort what was written into that which could not be recognized as truth; many do the same today as they scan God's Word through the tinted lens of their culture, transient bias, or closed minds. By and large if we had lived at that time we would have been prejudiced and pinned the label of strict legalist on all of them. Obeying the law was the forte for most. But would we have been wrong for some of them? Or perhaps we could be wrong about many of them.

John quotes Christ as saying, *"If you believed Moses you would believe me"* (Jn 5:46). And if they believed Moses, did they not truly know God? If they heeded the prophets, had they not learned from God? If they listened to the Psalms of David and recited and sang praises to the Lord, might not some of them have been faithful to God? Were there none that believed?

Who were most of the Hebrew people expecting? Was He not the One promised by God? Questions run rampant through the Gospels about whether Christ is the Messiah, the King of the Jews. Do none of those that question know God and claim His promises? Where did the palm waving crowds come from that hailed Him as King on His humble entrance to Jerusalem a week before that day of the cross? Did none of them believe or know God before Christ came on the scene?

The Greatest Old Testament Prophet

God planned that there would be large numbers primed, ready and waiting for the Messiah. Revival had spread across the land. God had been doing a unique and powerful work through His voice in the wilderness. Christ said that John the Baptist was the greatest man borne of woman, and the greatest prophet till that time (Mt 11:7-12). That includes the like of Moses, Elijah, Elisha, Isaiah, Jeremiah, and a host of others.

God sent John the Baptist to prepare the way for Christ. He preached that people should repent and seek the forgiveness of God. He helped turn people to God (Lk 1:16-17) and he announced the soon to come chosen One of God. And he anointed Him through baptism saying, *"Behold, the Lamb of God who takes away the sin of the world!"* (Jn 1:29).

Did this mighty and one of a kind prophet know God? Still, he sent his own followers to ask Christ, *"Are you the Expected One, or shall we look for someone else"* (Mt 11:2-6)?

Great crowds flocked to the teaching of John the Baptist. God was doing a great work. Among them were a number of Christ's disciples who first followed and studied under this prophet. All the Gospel writers praise and honor his work; Christ did as well.

Those who knew that they were sinners came to John in the wilderness; they acknowledged that their only hope was the mercy of God. They confessed that God's demand for righteousness far exceeded anything that they could do of themselves; they could never undo what they had done nor change the nature of their soul. And the OT prophet taught that God loves sinners and forgives those who repent. Who wouldn't love God knowing His mercy? Who wouldn't come to the One Who is the source of mercy? Which of them would not look for the promised One of God who was to take away the sin of the world?

Matthew says that the harlots and tax-gatherers believed John the Baptist (Mt 21:32). Luke says many people and tax-gatherers were baptized by John (Lk 7:29). John the disciple, wrote, *"He came as a witness, to testify about the Light, so that*

all might believe through him" (Jn 1:7). He touched many lives
with his work in the desert and Jordan valley. He prepared the
way.

Christ spoke to the multitudes that came to Him and asked,
*"What did you go out into the wilderness to see? A reed shaken
by the wind? But what did you go out to see? A man dressed in
soft clothing? Those who are splendidly clothed and live in
luxury are found in royal palaces! But what did you go out to
see? A prophet? Yes, I say to you, and one who is more than a
prophet"* (Lk 7:24b-26).

Now to the main point, did those who came to John the
Baptist believe and know God?   All were sinners and John
taught repentance.   Did they wait for the Messiah?   With no
reservation in the least, some believed God and waited for the
One to come.   But all these events took place shortly before or
during the early days of Christ's ministry. They had yet to know
and come to believe in Christ.

From the record in the four Gospels we know too that many
in the land did not heed the voice of John the Baptist. Among
these were the Pharisees and the lawyers (Lk 7:30), and the chief
priests and the elders of the people (Mt 21:23-32). They are the
ones who do not believe God, those who do not want to do
God's will. They saw no need to repent. Jesus said they had no
remorse. In their minds they saw no need for a Savior; for they
claimed they were "righteous" by their works.

They knew the Law and kept the commands outwardly while
their hearts were far from God. But their law keeping was not
the righteousness of God; they fell far short.

They should have listened to Christ and His Sermon on the
Mount (Mt 5:1-7:27).   Then they would have known that the
inward heart is what matters; at the very root and core we are all
dreadfully wicked and alienated from God. Good works will
never make us right before Him; we need the cross and the

power of a life giving cure. We need to be born again by the Spirit of God (Jn 3:5-8).

The reach of John the Baptist went far beyond the waters of the Jordan River. Many who study the Word think that he was the one who had plowed the field and sowed the seed among the Samaritans. We observe what Christ said to the disciples in Samaria, *"For in this case the saying is true, 'One sows and another reaps.' I sent you to reap that for which you have not labored; others have labored and you have entered into their labor"* (Jn 4:37-38). Christ and the disciples reaped what had been sown.

The woman at the well knew that the Messiah was more than a hoped for fantasy (Jn 4:25). A high noon meeting by a well of water taught her about God the Father and the One He sent. She was not a social pariah to Christ; she was a lost soul. The One with authority told her that God in Heaven is no respecter of persons. He seeks those who will worship Him in spirit and in truth. And God was seeking her and those in her city.

But did some prior herald of good news first reach out to the Samaritans? She and her town folk must have heard about the soon to come Messiah from someone. Note that the woman went into the city and boldly asked, *"This is not the Christ, is it"* (Jn 4:29)? Then the people were moved to go to this Man who told all. There were no stunning miracles, just the sign of His knowing all things, His soul-piercing Word, and then a fruitful harvest.

Had those of that city heard the message of the one down in the Jordan valley, the forerunner of Christ, called by God to do this special work? Or maybe they had read the texts of the OT and learned that the Messiah was to come? Some of them seemed to think that God was about to fulfill His promise to send His chosen One. Yet, without doubt, they had yet to recognize and honor Christ as the One that had been sent.

We have still more from the record of Scripture that attests to the reach of John the Baptist. His influence went far beyond the borders that edged his native land. Luke states that a man who had once followed John the Baptist was in Ephesus; his name was Apollos, a man born in Egypt (Acts 18:25). We learn too that Paul found at least twelve more disciples of this prophet in that far place. Paul baptized them into Christ on his third mission trip (Acts 19:1-7), a good number of years after the days of Christ on earth. At that late date they still had not heard that the Christ had come; but all were prepared for Him.

Why do we need to concede that there were many people who had turned to God during the ministry of John the Baptist? When we get to the Gospel of John we will understand. This fact alone may influence the way we should read the Scriptures; it could affect how we think of the day and work of Christ while with us on earth. This fact in turn, along with others dealt with here, may change the way we interpret what Paul and the Gospel authors wrote.

From such events we may find that we need to think anew about how God saves people. We may learn to see the order of salvation, *ordo salutis*, in a new light; the work of God that has been in sharp dispute for hundreds of years. Above all for this study, we intend to keep in our crosshairs the Scriptural meaning of the term "God's elect." But we have a ways to go.

Expectations of the Messiah

Most who study the Gospels get the distinct impression that the people of that day had little more than a foggy notion of what to expect from the One promised by God. They thought He was to come from the lineage of David; and He would restore the longed for kingdom. Most were hoping against hope that Roman rule would be tossed out of their land on its derrière. Even those close to Christ were slow to grasp the truth; they did so only by His direct teaching.

Those who knew the Sacred Scrolls thought He would be the prophet that would be like Moses (Dt 18:15-18). Most knew He was to do great works that only God could do (Is 55:11). And the Gospel writers confirm that He did do those works.

Still, we fail to find any from among the twelve that knew that Christ was going to die. Nor do we get the least trace of a hint that any knew that in His death He would shed His blood for the sins of the world. Peter, of all those who should have known, resisted the Lord when He said that He would soon die (Mt 16:21-23). Peter and his colleagues, were more prone to fight and take the sword to a few ears (Lk 22:49-50).

Now perhaps there were a few astute masters of the Sacred Scrolls in the land of that day who knew about Isaiah 53. That passage clearly tells us that the Servant would suffer greatly on our behalf. But those close to Him seemed to be in the dark; they acted in ways that tell us that they were clueless about God's plan of the cross for His Son.

Further, I do not read of any flash of brilliance in the NT that tells us that they knew Christ would rise from the dead. This was so despite the texts in the OT that pointed to that end. Even when Christ told them they failed to grasp that this world changing moment was about to burst upon them.

We do not find the disciples with much courage during the night of the mock trial, the hours on the cross, and then the three days while Christ was in the tomb. I suspect that their hope was shattered; the emptiness and blackness of death had begun to ravage the living, notwithstanding the fact that they had seen Christ raise the dead. Of all people they should have believed. But their treasury of truth had yet to come to the full light of day. And we would have been just like them.

The question for us to ponder is, before Christ taught them did they expect the Messiah to be Deity? Did they have any idea that they were to put their trust in Him as they did in God? Where would they have gotten that idea from the Scriptures they knew? Though well seasoned by the OT they could only see through a glass darkly. They only had brief glimpses in the Word about Who He was. The full revelation of what God was going to do was difficult for all to grasp at that time; though the truth was coming to pass before their very eyes and ears.

Some came to acknowledge His Deity, but only as Christ taught and lived before them. Perhaps those who had been with John the Baptist might have gathered this too. We don't know exactly what the prophet taught about the Messiah, though he did say that Christ would be the Lamb to take away the sin of the world (Jn 1:29). How many understood how this would take place? Once again, many questions are not answered in the Word.

Does any of the above add up to a mite of a difference? Yes, I find it highly suspect that anyone in that day would have thought that they should have faith in Christ as a starting point for their relationship with God. That would have been beyond foreign to them. In fact they would have been horror-struck by such a thought; this would have been out and out idolatry to them. And we know that the Hebrew people rightly eschewed false gods from the time of their 70-year exile; they had learned their lesson at the hand of God the hard way.

So, how were these people going to put their faith in Christ in the same way that they believed God? And if they truly knew God before, then the problem becomes a spiritual and mind boggling mystery. Would God have them make two decisions for salvation? And if they did not put their faith in Christ they would not be saved.

The spiritual and theological questions faced by the disciples and Paul must have been huge. What was God doing? How do they make sense of this? What was their thinking on the *ordo salutis*? How are Christ and the One Who sent Him linked in salvation? What did Christ say about this? And still more, what Words would the Holy Spirit give to them in order to express what was taking place? And for us today, does the Word of the NT even speak to these issues?

Did the NT authors ever make sense of the mystery? We will try to work through what the servants of God wrote. We will not be able to do so in full until we get to Romans, though there are many priceless clues along the way. These clues in the Word will help us stay on target until we get there. Then we can expect that God's chosen scholar on doctrine, the Apostle Paul, to have much to say about what happens to bring us to Christ.

Men of Israel in every city

We should also ponder the large crowds in the Holy City at the time of Pentecost? The numbers are not a few, and they came *"from every nation under heaven."* Luke states that they were *"devout men"* at that (Acts 2:5): Parthians, Medes, Elamites, Arabs, residents of Mesopotamia, Cappadocia, Pontus, Asia, Phrygia, Pamphylia, Egypt, Libya, Rome, and Crete. Did none of them hold to the faith of Abraham before Peter preached the Gospel? And Peter said, *"God has made Him both Lord and Christ—this Jesus whom you crucified"* (Acts 2:36).

We should not be surprised by the large numbers in the Holy City. Edersheim (1886, translated 1993), in "The Life and Times of Jesus the Messiah" and Tenny (2004), in "New Testament Times" both state that during the days of Christ on earth there were fewer Jews in Palestine than there were scattered throughout the known world. They got their numbers from sources such as Josephus and Philo. These secular Jewish writers from those days told of many clusters of Jews dispersed to the East and to the West of Israel at the time of Christ and Paul.

Those from far-off lands often made pilgrimages to the city of the one and only temple, and the largest crowds came for the Passover week. Tenny (2004) quotes Josephus who said that there were about 2.7 million Jews at one of these annual events during the time that the Emperor Nero was on the throne. This would have been about the same time that Paul was on trial in Rome. The Jewish author may have had cause to inflate the count; but in any case, the crowds must have been immense.

In that day there were two distinct groups that made up the Jewish culture. They were called the Hebrew people and the Hellenists. The Hebrew people were those in Palestine and on to the East, with large numbers in the area of present day Iraq. The Hellenists were the Jewish people to the West. They made their homes in such places as Egypt, Greece, and Rome, all under the prior influence of the Greeks, and later under Rome. From the book of Acts we know that there was at times a sharp rift between the Jews of East and West (Acts 6:1).

In the Middle East of Paul's day there were two major cities that served as melting pots for dispersed Jew and native Gentile. The historians above say that there may have been upwards of a million Jews that made their home in Egypt at the time of Christ; by far the largest enclave lived in the city of Alexandria. They wielded much influence across the Roman Empire from that metropolis of learning and commerce. And Antioch, we know from Acts, was the seat of the first full-scale outreach for Christ to the Gentiles. The church grew quite rapidly in that city under the charge of Paul and Barnabas (Acts 11).

Too, Edersheim estimates from studied sources that there may have been 40,000 Jews in Rome at the time of Augustus who ruled at the time of Christ's birth. He thought their numbers grew to about 60,000 at the time of Tiberius who governed about the time of Christ's public ministry. This historian found evidence of at least seven known synagogues in Rome from that day.

While most Gentiles did not warm to the Jews, historians claim that for the most part the Caesars treated them well (Edersheim, 1886, translated 1993). Many Jews first went to Rome as slaves, but were later freed. There was no law to ban Judaism from Rome except for a brief few years under Tiberius in 19 AD and then under Claudius in 41-54 AD. Priscilla and Aquila left Rome during the last period (cf Acts 20) and met up with Paul.

By the time Paul arrived in Rome as a prisoner, about 60-64 AD, many Jews had returned to the city. The numbers that made Rome their home then reached into the thousands. Luke states (Acts 28:23) that not a few came to hear what Paul had to say about the Christian "sect" that they had heard about. He may have had their willing and eager ear since he had sent a letter to them a few years before.

The secular record does not stand alone as evidence of the distant reach of the Jewish way of life. In the book of Acts, Luke reports that Judaism had set root across the known world (Acts 15:21). At an early Church Council in Jerusalem, James, the Lord's half-brother, said that there were synagogues in all cities since ancient times. And the mission trips by Paul and his troupe confirm that this was so for most major cities under the rule of Rome.

The synagogues of the dispersed Jews seem to have had an open door policy for Gentiles. Paul found proselytes and those who feared God in all the cities where he went. The Jews had touched many lives over the years. In a few places in Acts, Luke says there were more than a few Gentiles in the synagogues (Acts 14:1; 17:4; 17:12) and they were hearing the Word of the OT before Paul went there. Had any turned from idols to the true and living God? Or was their worship all a sham?

From the Gospel of Matthew we know what Christ said about the proselytes. He told the Scribes and Pharisees that they go over land and sea to get one new convert and then they make him more of a *"son of hell"* than what they were (Mt 23:15). His statement attests that most of these former pagans fell far short of knowing God. They became nothing more than religious zealots; still, would that have held true for each and every last one of them?

We will take a close look at this question as we explore the book of Acts and Paul's letters. We must keep this in mind as we read about the people to whom Paul and Barnabas gave the Gospel of God.

Luke tells us in his record that some of those that Paul met even worshipped God (cf Acts 16:14 and 18:7). Was Luke confused? Did he stretch the truth of what he saw and heard? We read the texts that speak of these incidents and since the events are in the NT we think, "Oh, there's someone who worships God; but they don't know Him." Yet who are we to say? Might not some of them been true to God while most were falsely pious, just as was the case in Israel?

If we had read that same profile in the OT we would have assumed right or wrong, "Oh, there is an OT saint." And we gloss over the fact that they only had the OT Scriptures in those first years. And we ignore the obvious that few outside of the land of Palestine had heard that Christ had come. And this was still so on Paul's third mission trip, as we shall see when we take a close look at the book of Acts.

Why is this brief review of the first years of the Church age important? We know that there were those who believed God in the land of Palestine. But if the dispersed Jews were greater in number, should we be so naïve as to conclude that there were none among the scattered who did as well? Did God confine His work to the land of Palestine before the advent of Christ?

Where did the Magi come from? We can only ponder the thought. But we do know that in those days there were many Hebrew people to the East in the area of the Tigris and Euphrates rivers, and beyond. Some 500 plus years before the NT was written Daniel had been made the chief of all the wisemen, the magi, in that region (Dn 2:48). Perhaps the nexus is thin, but where would the Magi have gotten the idea that a king was to be born to the Jews at about the time of Christ's birth? Recall that Daniel was the one who had the time of His first coming nailed down (Dn 9).

Not all of the Hebrew people returned home from their exile to that foreign land. Might there have been a true witness in that far region to the East over the many years that had gone by? Tongue in cheek, I assume that God sought those who would worship Him out among the scattered too.

In Acts 8:26-39 we find a surprise visitor to the Holy City, and he wasn't a Jew. The Ethiopian eunuch was high up in the court of his Queen. He had gone to worship in a far country, to the temple in the Holy City. Was their OT truth being taught in the land of Ethiopia?

We can only guess, tongue in cheek, that the Eunuch might have been an OT saint, and no doubt the first and last one in all of Africa. Yet, we know of a second such man 600 plus years before. He pulled a prophet of God from the miry mud of a deep pit (Jer 38:7-13; 39:16-18). Did that man from Jeremiah's day return to his native land and spread the Word? The OT prophet said that the eunuch of that former day trusted the Lord. And the record says he survived the onslaught of God's wrath by the arm of Babylon against the land of Judah and the Holy City.

How dare we assume that God had none left for His name among the men of Israel or among the Gentiles across the known world? He would not have had many, as the vast majority of those who thought they knew God would have been just like the people in Palestine. But after study I would never want to claim that God's Word had failed in all places but for a small handful in the land of promise. Yet that is how we typically read the NT. Could we be wrong?

I have come to realize that there were a few faithful to God's name in many places. Paul describes those that were Jews as the *"children of the promise"* (Rom 9:8). They maintained OT faith in God. They looked for the Messiah, not knowing what to expect; and not knowing He had come until they were told.

And these keepers of the promise had touched many of those around them. Their witness was not a futile waste since God worked through them to reach others. Among them and in their places of worship we find many Gentiles who had at one time basked and boasted in false gods. Paul's travels confirm this to be so.

A few of these Gentiles had come to know and love God. They had turned from the delusion of decorated scarecrows (Jer 10) to the God of Abraham. When we read that there were those who worshiped God, I believe the words are written correctly. They also looked for the Messiah. They knew there was One to come. But they too would not know what to expect.

Old Testament Scriptures only

As we read the NT today we seldom pause to remember the fact that the books of the NT did not exist at the time of Christ. Nor did Paul have the NT on his three mission trips. And the NT was not known to any of the first readers of his letters. And beyond this, Paul's letters, when first received by an infant church, would not have yet been seen as part of the Sacred Scrolls.

Hence, in the day that Paul wrote his letters they had nothing more than the books of the OT to read and study as declared and certain truth, along with one or two letters from Paul. We should not dismiss this critical fact when we try to get our minds around what Paul wrote. The leaders in those churches would also have known what Paul said when he was with them in person. From Luke's report in Acts, Paul always started with the OT when he taught in the synagogues. He never failed to tell of God as portrayed in their Sacred Scrolls.

When most of us study the NT today we tend to skip from book to book. We get a broader view of what was happening at that time. But once we grow up we seldom wear out the pages of anything that comes before Matthew. But if we only had one letter, and little else other than the OT, I think we would have read the letters from Paul in a much different way.

To put perspective on this, consider the situation of their day. Most of the people where Paul went had 39 books of the OT that told them about God and His promises. Many would have thought that they were firmly grounded in the Word.

Then a man that they had never met came to their town for three to four weeks (the time was much longer in a few places). This man claimed that he was sent by God to teach them about a risen Lord Who had conquered the grave and went to heaven. Some time after he left they then receive one or two short letters from him, but they had yet to see or claim those short letters as penned by God. How would that frame the context of what they knew and how they reasoned? Would their theology be the same as ours?

Those who left the synagogue to join the small group of believers would have thought about and read about the One Who sent the Messiah in a much more prominent and fixed way. Most were studied Jews; or if Gentile, they had been attracted by and immersed in Jewish teaching. If taught well they knew of God's promise of One to come.

They saw God through eyes fixed by the lens of the OT, not so much through a mindset guided by reading all the books of the NT. How would this affect what Paul and the disciples wrote and taught? Would this not influence how the people read Paul's epistles? When we get to the Scriptures we will think more on this. But we must not forget that whatever the apostles wrote, the truth was from God; and we are called upon to shape our minds from what He has said.

I would think that the people of that day would have asked a number of very searching and significant questions. How is this NT faith different than my OT faith? How is this new faith the same? Did Paul speak to this? Did the Disciples? Did Christ? And if they did, and I will show that they did when we get to the Scriptures, what do they say? And more, is there anything about this that has relevance to the debate about who the elect are, and hence to the question about free will?

Suffice for now; send up a red flag on these crucial observations. Bring them to mind as we go through the texts to come, as we will soon feast on the truths of Scripture. In the end you may disagree, but at least you will need to weigh a strong third option that will challenge both the Calvin' and Arminius' schools of thought on God's elect. And more, this new option will have much to say about free will.

When I came to grips with the self-evident fact that they had little more than the OT in the first years of the church era, I then tried to read the texts of the NT in like manner. I put myself in the sandals of those from that day. I found that many of the Scriptures become more lucid and less awkward. Quite often when Paul and John write about belief and faith they are talking about God, the One Who sent Christ, not just faith in Christ. And often they write about both. This will make a difference in how we read Paul's epistles.

Some might insist that believing God and faith in Christ are the same thing. But Paul and other NT writers make a distinction. When we get to the Scriptures I will point out when they do. Some of the texts come alive with fresh thoughts and illumination when we read from this perspective.

Distribution of the OT throughout the known world

Here is one more obvious fact that most students of the Word pay rare heed as they search through and try to derive truths from the books of the NT.

The seed of the Word found in the OT was sown far and wide among the Hebrew and Hellenistic Jews, in all cities of the Roman world (cf Acts 15:21). We have seen that this is borne out by Paul's visits to many places where he found men of Israel, proselytes, and those who feared God. They all met on the Sabbath Day for teaching and worship; the Scrolls of the OT were the center of study each time.

God's Word does not return to Him void. Although the Jews were well-known for twisting what was written by Moses and the prophets, can we say that there were none that responded to the Word in the manner of Abraham? Were there none that truly followed Moses? Were there none that had learned from the prophets? Were there none that looked for the Messiah? Were there none that truly believed God?

There is still more profundity to the spread of God's Word in those days. When Ptolemy II reigned in Egypt from 285 to 246 BC, some 280 plus years before Paul's mission trips, the OT was translated into the Koiné Greek, the language of the common people throughout the Middle East. And this Greek text, known as the Septuagent, became the favored version that was used and studied across the Roman world. Does this not say how important the Sacred Scrolls were to them?

Edersheim, in the late 1800's, stated that the Septuagent became the Bible favored by the people. He claims that the purchase of a copy was well within the reach of many due to cheap slave labor to do the copying. We know though that the masses still did not have the Scrolls in their hands, except on the Sabbath. Yet with the advent of this version of the Bible text the Hellenistic Jews heard and studied the Word in their best-known language. We all can appreciate the value of having the Word read and taught in a language that makes the most sense to us.

We cannot be certain that the Greek text was read on the Sabbath of those days. But most likely both the Greek and Hebrew would have been, at least in the Roman world. And I ask once again, does God's Word fail to bear fruit?

No doubt, many study the Bible over a complete lifetime and yet never believe. Most didn't in those days either. But does that mean none would? To claim that the Word is that impotent seems close to ludicrous. By tradition, that is how we think when we dig into the texts of the NT, especially the book of Acts. Should we not have more confidence in the Word of God in the OT than that?

The distribution of the Greek translation of the OT Scriptures had another profound and far-reaching affect on the world of that day. Not only could the Hellenistic Jews read in their best known language, but the Gentiles could as well. And most of the people where Paul went spoke in Greek. They had heard the Word from God read in their native tongue. By and large they went to the synagogue for this very reason? Few would have been there on the Sabbath if the meetings were held in Hebrew or Aramaic; but Greek, yes.

And what would the Gentiles learn from the Word taught in the synagogue? Would they have tried to adhere to the greatest commandment? Would they have listened when they were told that all the nations of the world would be blessed through the descendent of Abraham? Did none come to know that God worked through the Jewish nation and people? Had none of them faithfully turned from their idol worship of the past? In fact, might the Word in Greek been part of the reason so many Gentiles gave up their false gods? Who does Paul reach in the Gentile world for the most part? Luke states that they were Greeks!

Men who wrote the New Testament

There were at least eight, perhaps nine men who wrote NT books, all of which were Jews, save one. The one exception, Luke, spent much of his time under Paul's mentoring. These men were all saturated by an OT mindset. They had nothing more than the OT Scriptures, Christ's teaching, and the Holy Spirit to guide their thinking.

Their mindset alone should warn us to take extra caution. They wrote for their day and to the populace that concerned them. So if possible we should interpret with the wisdom and knowledge of their day. They wrote the words of God under the control of the Holy Spirit. But God is not capricious; His voice through His servants that went before has a direct bearing for how we should read the NT today.

I will not say more about this basic contextual given for now, but we must try to think in terms of their point of view as they receive new revelation about what God was doing. Their mindset can teach us much for how we need to understand the NT Scriptures.

Summary of Chapter Two

To sum up, we tend to misjudge the years of transition from OT to NT and those who lived in that day. And the further Paul traveled from the Promised Land the more likely we are to misperceive what was taking place. We see those that Paul reached as monotheists, legalists, and Judaizers who did not know God. And for the most part, they fit these genera.

But some would have truly believed God. In this regard we are remiss in how we handle the Word. We fail to think like those in that day, and I doubt that we read the texts as Paul and the Gospel writers intended. From our careless assumptions we misconstrue who the elect were and are. And we fail to see how God worked then and likewise how He still works today.

We must put the NT Scriptures into their proper setting to attain an exegesis that fits. A few basic facts from that early era add much weight to what I will share in the next chapters. There we will dig into the texts at the heart of the debate about the elect and free will.

Let's review these basic facts. Many of the Hebrew people in Palestine at the time of Christ truly believed God before Christ came on the scene. The proof is in the power of God's Word, and seen foremost by the revival through the voice of God spoken by John the Baptist. Many expected the Messiah, yet He was an enigma. Few if any knew that they were to put their faith in Him as they did in God.

Also, as we study the Spirit inspired words of Paul we must take note that more Jews lived outside of Palestine than in the land. Synagogues were common to most cities of the empire of Rome; and the OT was read every Sabbath. Many Gentiles gathered with the Jews on the Sabbath; and they had heard and read the Word in their own language for over 200 years.

I too failed to see how the above facts of that day might affect the way we read the Scriptures. We must take these into account. Such is part of the meat of hermeneutics. Doctrines we hold today can suffer without a proper grasp of the era of those first days of faith in Christ. Thus I have written this chapter now and not later.

Lest you conclude too soon from this chapter, that I think God's elect are OT saints, that is not the case. No doubt though, OT saints are a huge clue that will help us identify who the elect are.

Chapter Three

Gospel of John and His Epistles

We can now take our plunge into the depths and riches of the Word of God, but we must look through the lens of pre-NT days. First we will examine the main texts in the Gospel of John, those at the heart of the debate. Most of these are what Calvin scholars use as a base for some of their doctrine. If read alone with no regard to another way to explain these texts I could agree with how they interpret them. But then I will add a few more Scriptures from John that they ignore. These will lead us to a much different conclusion.

There are at least eight key passages in John that strict Calvinists use to support their view of "elect then faith." The list is not exhaustive, but these will help us get started.

Jn 1:13 -- "who were born, not of blood nor of the will of the flesh nor of the will of man, but of God."

Jn 6:37 -- "All that the Father gives Me will come to Me, and the one who comes to me I will certainly not cast out."

Jn 6:44 -- "No one can come to Me unless the Father who sent Me draws him: and I will raise him up on the last day."

Jn 6:65 -- "And He was saying, 'For this reason I have said to you, that no one can come to Me unless it has been granted him from the Father.'"

Jn 8:47 -- "He who is of God hears the words of God; for this reason you do not hear them, because you are not of God."

Jn 10:26-29 -- "But you do not believe because you are not of My sheep. My sheep hear My voice, and I know them, and they follow Me; and I give eternal life to them, and they will never perish; and no one will snatch them out of My hand. My Father, who has given them to Me, is greater than all; and no one is able to snatch them out of the Father's hand."

Jn 12:37-41 -- "But though He had performed so many signs before them, yet they were not believing in Him. This was to fulfill the word of Isaiah the prophet, which he spoke: 'Lord, who has believed our report? And to whom has the arm of the Lord been revealed?' For this reason they could not believe, for Isaiah said again, 'He has blinded their eyes and He hardened their heart, so that they would not see with their eyes and perceive with their heart, and be converted and I heal them.' These things Isaiah said because he saw His glory, and he spoke of Him."

Jn 17:6 -- "I have manifested Your name to the men whom You gave me out of the world; they were Yours, and You gave them to Me, and they have kept Your word."

Interpreting the Scriptures

The above brief texts seem to support the idea that God is in complete control; we do nothing other than receive what God gives to us. None of the verses actually say this but the intimation is that God the Father gives the faith to be saved. He is the One who gives people to Christ, not that people choose to believe in Christ. So they are God the Father's to give. And the text of John 1:13 is rich and more than clear; we are born again with faith in Christ by the will of God, not by the will of man (Jn 6:37-44).

John quotes Christ as saying that God the Father draws people to Christ. <u>All that the Father gives Him will come to Him</u> and they <u>cannot come unless the Father draws them</u>. And there are those that cannot even hear the words of God since they do not belong to God (Jn 8:47).

Another text says that people do not believe because they are not of Christ's sheep. In other words we have to be one of the sheep before we can believe in Christ. If salvation in Christ is a choice, a matter of free will, then belief in Christ should come before being one of the sheep? When Christ speaks the sheep hear His voice and they follow Him. But they are already one of the sheep (Jn 10:26-29).

Taken as a whole these passages are substantially convincing that God does it all; His grace is sovereign and cannot be resisted. He has chosen a flock of sheep from among all the people of the earth; and they all follow Christ. They all believe in Him. The key point is that their belief in Christ comes after being a sheep. That is what those who adhere to Calvin precepts teach. What could be more certain from these texts?

Scholars who defend free will see these Scriptures from a different perspective, vague as their exegesis may be. But I think the Calvin view is correct. God the Father does give people to the Son. And I also think the sheep are Christ's sheep before they believe in Christ. The Scriptures are very clear and I do not think this can be argued, lest we twist and distort what God has said.

Yet, a major problem still exists. Calvin scholars have not seen a vital piece to the puzzle in John. The flaw erodes, in part, three of the five basic tenets that extreme Calvinists hold, and it eliminates a fourth. The flaw pervades much of how they see the texts in question, not only in the Gospel of John but elsewhere throughout the NT, as we shall see.

But Calvinists are not alone in failing to see the critical flaw. So do those who hold to a boundless free will. Neither camp has adequately wrestled with the texts to fit all the pieces in place. And the debate has been going on for 400 plus years. We too often let our dogma guide how we think and how we read a text. And the way strict free will scholars see these texts leads to problems in how they interpret Scriptures elsewhere.

The missing piece of the puzzle stares us in the face. The flaw is so obvious it is almost painful to see how theologians have missed a key factor all these years.

Those in the days of Christ, and a few years after, who only had the Word of the OT to study, would have quickly seen the problem in the texts of John's Gospel. The crowds that followed John the Baptist would have seen the problem. All with the faith of Abraham in that day would have been stunned by what we omit today.

And the Pharisees came close to seeing the issue and they seethed with anger. They thought they were the one's that belonged to God since they were descendents of Abraham. And they said that they were the righteous ones because they kept the Law and they thought they did good works. But while they heard Christ correctly in that they did not belong to God, they missed the point just as most students of the Word do today.

So what is the option? What is the missing piece of the perplexing debate? Since most Calvin scholars fail to see this I must be cautious about any claim to be right. And I must be doubly cautious since free will scholars are not prone to explain the texts in the way I will describe. In fact they may have just as much trouble with what I will say here as the strict Calvinists.

The Elect in the Gospel of John

Now to the thesis for what I write; most all theologians of a Calvin persuasion think that the people drawn by God the Father to Christ in the sixth chapter of John are the elect. I agree with this. They also think that the sheep already belong to Christ before they believe in Him. These are also the elect of that day. I agree with this too.

Where we part company is that these elect know and believe God. They belong to God by faith and they are already sheep. They have not yet believed in Christ. But if they do not truly believe God they are not sheep, and God the Father will not give them to Christ. They will not be born again with faith in Christ.

Hard to grasp? Let me make the case. Let's start with the sheep passage in John 10.

> Jn 10:25-30 -- "Jesus answered them, 'I told you, and you do not believe; the works that I do in My Father's name, these testify of Me, But you do not believe, because you are not of My sheep. My sheep hear My voice, and I know them, and they follow Me; and I give eternal life to them, and they shall never perish: and no one is able to snatch them out of My hand. My Father, who has given them to Me, is greater than all; and no one is able to snatch them out of the Father's hand. I and the Father are One.'"

One slice of evidence is in the last sentence; *"I and the Father are one."* Now if the sheep belong to the Father could they belong on the basis of faith in God? And since Christ is one with God, the sheep simply recognize Christ for Who He is, for they *"hear His voice"* and they follow Him. Those that do not believe God will not recognize Him for they do not believe God.

We need to bear in mind that for people who only had the OT, their faith began by believing God the Father, not Christ. But if the sheep do not believe God then they may not be Christ's sheep. In fact even today, might we need to have true faith in God before we can recognize Who Christ is and believe in Him? Here is faith to faith.

John teaches that the only flock that Christ will have are those who truly believe God. Can God the Father, the One Who sent Christ, have one flock of sheep and Christ another? Can we believe in the Lamb of God without believing in the One Who sent the Lamb? Can we believe in the One Who is the answer to our sin problem before we believe God when He tells us we have a sin problem that alienates us from Himself?

Anyone that truly believed God in that day would indeed hear Christ's voice and believe Him. He and the Father are One. And there were large numbers in that day who already knew God, rather God knew them.

So might God the Father give people to Christ on the condition that they believe Him, the One Who sent Christ. And the One in the flesh will not manifest Himself to none but those who truly believe God. On the other hand those that do not know, have faith in God He blinds so that they do not see Who Christ is. Christ dies for all that truly believe the One Who sent Him, and hence they belong to God just as Abraham did. We must remember that Christ is Immanuel, God with us, but we will not recognize the One with us if we don't know the One that sent Him.

In other words, no true belief in God = no belief in God the Son. Could this be what Jesus taught and John reports? Might this explain statements in John such as, *"My sheep hear my voice?" "You cannot come to me unless the Father draws you." "You do not believe because you are not of my sheep." "No one can come to me unless drawn by My Father."*

The way John develops the theme of belief in his Gospel speaks to this premise. We will try to track some of his thought as we move through what he writes. This view will challenge the way we most often interpret Christ's work on earth. And this will also lead to rethinking what Paul and others wrote.

Witnesses and Believers

There is one needed condition that is required for this view of the elect to hold water. The Scriptures must show that there were many in the land that had already believed God when Christ came on the scene to disclose His work on earth.

And yes, the Scriptures confirm this to be so. There were more than a few; and most likely great numbers, in that day and land that already had true faith in God. Doubtful, you think? Study again.

How can we be certain? John reports this to be so with great press and acclaim, on the front page of Chapter One of his Gospel. A revival had just cut across all corners of the land and touched the hearts of many people. Crowds flocked to the wilderness. John the Baptist had done the work that God called him to do. And if people accepted the message of John the Baptist they would have believed God; and they would also soon believe in Christ.

John the disciple writes about that work in the desert.

Jn 1:6-7 -- "There came a man sent from God, whose name was John. He came as a witness, to testify about the Light, so that all might believe through Him."

The ministry of John the Baptist was well known throughout the land. He was the talk of the country. His witness and message went all the way to the top, to the stuffed shirts of Jerusalem (Jn 1:19-20); and they sent the local religious CIA to investigate who he was.

Even those who ruled on behalf of Rome were provoked and cut to the quick by his words (Lk 3:18-20). They would not yield to his strong censure of their grievous and well-known sin; for this cause they locked him behind prison walls and beheaded him. The work of God through this prophet touched the lives of many. All the Gospel writers validate this.

And the people of that day had more than the revival led by this one of a kind prophet; they also had the OT Scriptures. At least a few would have believed Moses and the former prophets, even if they had not heard the more recent voice of God in the wilderness. And these too had yet to recognize and believe Christ. God the Father would make certain that they did so. Yes, they were given to Christ. There is little doubt that no one could come to Christ unless they truly believed God.

In those days they knew enough to start with the belief of Abraham, who believed God. That's what their Sacred Scrolls said (Gn 15:6). Christ did not need to explain this in detail. But He certainly had to explain why people should or would come to and believe Him.

And the writers of the Gospels would have known the need to believe God as Abraham did. They did not need to write an appendage to the OT that told them the need to believe, trust, and love God. But they did need to explain why and how a person would or should believe in Christ.

A stack of evidence for this exegesis comes from the words of Christ Himself. He states that He had five witnesses that confirmed Who He was. He did not stand alone in His claim to be the Messiah. John writes about these other voices in the fifth chapter. Let me quote:

> Jn 5:31-47 -- "If I alone testify about Myself, My testimony is not true. There is another who testifies of Me, and I know that the testimony which He gives about Me is true. You have sent to John, and he has testified to the truth. But the testimony which I receive is not from man, but I say these things so that you may be saved. He was the lamp that was burning and was shining and you were willing to rejoice for a while in his light. But the testimony which I have is greater than the testimony of John; for the works which the Father has given Me to accomplish--the very works that I do—testify about Me, that the Father has sent Me. And the Father who sent Me, He has testified of Me. You have neither heard His voice at any time nor seen His form. You do not have His word abiding in you, for you do not believe Him whom He sent. You search the Scriptures because you think that in them you have eternal life; it is these that testify about Me; and you are unwilling to come to Me so that you may have life. I do not receive glory from men; but I know you, that you do not have the love of God in yourselves. I have come in My Father's name, and you do not receive Me; if another comes in his own name, you will receive him. How can you believe, when you receive glory from one another, and you do not seek the glory that is from the one and only God? Do not think that I will accuse you before the Father; the one who accuses you is Moses, in whom you have set your hope. For if you believed Moses, you would believe Me, for he wrote of Me. But if you do not believe his writings, how will you believe My words?'"

The five witnesses to Christ were John the Baptist, the OT Scriptures, His works, Moses, and God the Father. Some scholars say there are only four that witness as they combine Moses with the Scriptures. But there is more to the Scrolls of the OT than Moses.

And Christ's works were significant signs too; the OT foresaw that the Messiah would do certain kinds of works (Is 11:2, 35:5-6, 61:1). And still more, only God could do what Christ did. For this reason Christ told the disciples of John the Baptist to go tell the prophet about His works (Mt 11:2-6).

And those who did heed these witnesses would soon believe and follow Christ. All of them had already put their trust in God.

People who did not heed any of the witnesses had no true faith in God to begin with, and hence they would not believe in Christ. In fact Christ said that they had no love for God. I doubt then that they belonged to God. Hence God would not give them to His Son.

Why would John build a case for all the witnesses? Why did he give so much prominence to God's voice from the Jordan Valley? There must have been people around that had learned from God by what these witnesses said. So John put ink to the fact and by doing this he said that their claims about Christ were important. Their testimony meant something.

We cannot deny that God could give people to Christ by His arbitrary fiat alone in the absence of faith, if that were His plan. The fact is God could raise up true believers from the stones of a field, if He so desired (Mt 3:9). But I do not think that is what happens here. And there are more Scriptures that speak to this.

The fifth chapter of John comes before the contested verses of John chapter six. Each witness is of great value. But the most critical witness is God the Father. If we truly believe God and His Word then we have it made because God the Father then draws us to and gives us to Christ. In fact if we do not believe God we will never come to believe the Son. In other words only those who truly believe God will be born again by His will to have faith in Christ (Jn 1:13).

But are there other Scriptures in the Gospel of John to support this interpretation? Are those who believe God the ones He draws to faith in the Son? And more, can we connect faith in God to being one of the elect who will believe Christ, the second person of the Trinity.

We will leave the last question for a later chapter. For now we will focus our attention on the Gospel of John.

Study these verses in the Gospel of John to see if they weigh in to make "faith to faith" a viable option.

> Jn 5:24 -- "Truly, truly, I say to you, he who hears My word, and believes Him who sent Me, has eternal life, and does not come into judgment, but has passed out of death into life."

Christ speaks here and this passage also comes before the texts that Calvinists cling to for their base of support in the sixth chapter of John. How can the people in the verse quoted here have eternal life when nothing is said about faith in Christ? All they do is hear Christ's message and believe the One Who sent Christ.

In this verse we have the authoritative teaching of the Son of God that we still need to believe the One Who sent Him. We cannot ignore what He says. But does this make a difference? And if it does then what bearing does faith in the One Who sent Him have on faith in Christ?

In the era of the disciples which comes first? Would it not be God, the One Who sent Christ? Could they put their faith in the Lamb of God before they believed God? Can we?

Jn 5:46-47 -- "For if you believed Moses, you would
have believed Me: for he wrote about Me. But if you
do not believe his writings, how will you believe My
words?"

If they believed Moses, they knew God as well. But most
people in that day distorted what Moses said. They read into
him their own man-centered and error-prone ideas. Hence they
really did not adhere to what Moses taught. But Christ said that
if they had true belief in what Moses taught then they would
believe in Christ. In fact there is an air of certainty to His
statement that this would no doubt be so. And to the contrary, if
they did not believe Moses they would not believe Christ.

Jn 6:45 -- "It is written in the prophets, 'And they
shall all be taught of God.' Everyone who has heard
and learned from the Father, comes to me."

Many use this verse to teach the doctrine of "elect then
faith." But the statement is far stronger evidence for a prior
relationship with God, and that would have been based on
believing Him. For they not only had heard from God, they had
learned from the Father. Can anyone learn from God if they
don't believe Him?

Notice that this verse is placed squarely in the midst of the
passage that says the Father draws people to Christ. Without the
least bit of skepticism, if they had a faith relationship with God
then they had to be "handed over" or "drawn to" Christ. This is
not quite the same as God choosing to give people to Christ in an
arbitrary way.

Read another verse in John that those of a Calvin persuasion
use.

Jn 8:42 -- "Jesus said to them, 'If God were your
Father, you would love Me, for I proceeded forth and

have come from God, for I have not even come on My
own initiative, but He sent Me.'"

Those who had the faith of Abraham would hear these words
and say God is my Father because I know Him. I believe God,
and I love Him, I better believe in Christ and love Him too.
"God has sent Him."

On the other hand the falsely pious who heard Christ say
this, and yet rejected Him, would think that Christ was flat out
telling them that they did not know God. They were furious
about such blunt indictments; so they accused Him of all kinds
of things. They had put their confidence in their own works
rather than in God. They no doubt thought, "How dare a man
from Galilee make such claims?" This all the more suggests a
pregnant meaning here; not that God simply gives people to
Christ without the condition of true belief in He the Father.

Christ was saying that those who came to Him did belong to
God. And the sinners came! Many had come to God and
repented under John the Baptist's outreach. And many came
because of Christ's Words and they believed the One Who sent
Him. Everyone who came believed God and depended on His
mercy. But where was God's mercy and grace going to come
from?

Calvinists read the verse above to say that we belong to God
before there is faith. And if we belong to God, before we love
Christ then God the Father picked us with no condition, and He
gives us to Christ. In other words we are God's elect by His fiat
alone, not by faith.

But with "faith to faith" the statement speaks to a different
sense. We belong to God by faith. The faith is in the One Who
sent Christ. And so, if we believe God we will love Him and we
will love the Son of God too.

Compare the last paragraph and quoted verse with what the same NT author says in his first Epistle (1 Jn 5:1). There he writes too, that if you love the Father, you will love the Son. Once again the crux of the text points to a logical sequence of God the Father to God the Son. We must believe both.

The critical passage

> Jn 17:3 -- "This is eternal life, that they may know You, the only true God, and Jesus Christ whom You have sent."

Those who hold to "elect then faith" quote John 17:6 to bolster their view: *"I have manifested Your name to the men whom You gave Me out of the world; they were Yours and You gave them to Me, and they have kept Your word."* To take 17:6 out of the context of 17:3 makes it seem that God the Father gives people to Christ on no basis whatsoever.

This interpretation is serious error. The people given to the Son already know God. They "know" Him; God did not just know them. In fact, the quote from Christ Himself says that eternal life is to know both God and the Son of God.

In His priestly prayer Christ states four more times that we need to believe and know that God sent Him (Jn 17:8, 21, 23, 25). This strongly suggests that we cannot put our faith in Him unless we know He comes from God and that He is God with us. And what good is faith in Christ if we do not believe God and that He sent Him.

So how do all the pieces of the puzzle in the Gospel of John fit the mosaic? John says the Father has given all things into the Son's hands (Jn 3:35). And Matthew confirms that all things were handed over to Christ (Mt 11:27). Besides what else these words might indicate, they also suggest a "faith in God to a faith in Christ" sequence. These words do not suggest a "nothing to a faith in Christ" idea.

There is a marked contrast between the two views that will
come into play as we look to the book of Acts and Paul's
Epistles. I make a distinction here between Christ as one part of
the Godhead and God the Father as a different part, yet knowing
both are God. Still, people in that day did not fully grasp that the
Messiah was to be Deity, as well as fully man. Where would
they have gotten that idea? They did not even know that He
would rise from the dead (Jn 20:8-9).

People of that day could not resist the call to believe Christ if
they already knew God. But on the other hand the OT pages are
filled with people who reject God. God sent His servants over
and over yet most spurned the call from God to come to Him.

Jer 7:25-26a -- "Since the day that your fathers came
out of the land of Egypt until this day, I have sent you
all My servants the prophets, daily rising early and
sending them. Yet they did not listen to Me or incline
their ear, but stiffened their neck..."

Was the message of those He sent bogus? Is the call to
believe in the NT a sham? Did God choose His people before
faith, even faith in God the Father, Who is the foremost witness
to the Son (1 Jn 5:9-10)?

Let's take a close look at the most well known and prized
verse in the Bible.

Jn 3:16 -- "For God so loved the world, that He gave
His only begotten Son, that whoever believes in Him
should not perish, but have eternal life."

Should we even begin to think that we could believe in the
Son in this verse without believing the One Who sent the Son?
Would this not be absurd? However, if we have true faith in
God, will He keep the Son from us? Not on your life. I quote
once again, *"I and the Father are One."* Faith in Christ is
contingent on faith in God; this is part of the Gospel of God

taught by John the disciple. Christ, Who was God with us, came to do a wonderful work. He was acting on behalf of His own people, those that truly believe God and all those who would do so in the future.

This next verse the extreme Calvinists will not like.

Jn 14:1 -- "Do not let your heart be troubled; believe in God, believe also in me."

The context of this verse does not refer to salvation; rather Christ is talking to the disciples about going to heaven to prepare a place for those that belong to Him. Nonetheless, the pattern of faith to faith seems fairly clear. This is what was taking place all through Christ's earthly ministry.

John the Baptist

God's Word shows that certain people came to Christ under the condition that they already believed God. One that we need to review in brief was the last OT prophet. What do the Scriptures say?

Jn 1:32-33 -- "John testified saying, 'I have seen the Spirit descending as a dove out of heaven, and he remained on Him. And I did not recognize Him, but He who sent me to baptize in water said to me, 'He upon whom you see the Spirit descending and remaining upon Him, this is the One who baptizes in the Holy Spirit.'"

Would anyone say that John the Baptist had yet to believe God at this point in his life? No. He believed God and God revealed to Him the Son. Would God have done so if John the Baptist had not believed God already? I think not.

Of course we know that God chose John the Baptist before his birth to be a special prophet for Him (Lk 1:13-17). This would appear to make God in full control too. But if God can know who will believe Him before their birth He can choose anyone for a purpose to serve Him prior to their birth. We will discuss this in more detail later in the book.

Disciples as True Believers in God

There is not much doubt that the first few disciples also believed God before faith in Christ. Review John Chapter One to verify this. They had been with John the Baptist and had heard his voice. Then there was Nathaniel who was seen by the Lord as having no guile. What might he have been doing under the fig tree (Jn 1:48)? If some of the twelve believed God, how many more followers would have too?

But there was one that did not believe. John told us about this man whom God the Father did not grant permission to come. Why would God do such a thing, doesn't He want all to believe in Christ?

> Jn 6:64-65 -- "'But there are some of you who do not believe.' For Jesus knew from the beginning who they were who did not believe, and who it was that would betray Him. And He was saying, 'For this reason I have said to you, that no one can come to Me unless it has been granted him from the Father.'"

This man who follows Christ does not have true faith. This is the one who would betray the Son of God, and we know that he was Judas. John says this man was one of the twelve, but Christ knew he did not believe from the beginning. If he does not believe God, of course he cannot be one of the sheep that would follow Christ. We must remember that Christ is the Shepherd of God's people, and He is One with the Father.

I concede that this case falls far short of nailing down the premise, but the text suggests this pattern. Now let's go to a third case that fits in greater detail and adds more weight to the premise.

For this example we need to leave the Gospel of John for a moment and go to Matthew. There we find a passage that sheds more light on our path.

> Mt 16:15-17 -- "He said to them, 'But who do you say that I am?' Simon Peter answered, 'You are the Christ, the Son of the living God.' And Jesus said to him, 'Blessed are you, Simon Barjona, because flesh and blood did not reveal this to you, but My Father who is in heaven.'"

The intriguing part that we need to see is where Jesus tells Peter that the Father revealed to him that Christ was the Son of the living God. This statement runs parallel to what John reports in his sixth chapter (vs 37-47). Here we seem to have an instance that illustrates what John writes about. So God the Father does give people to the Son.

Albeit, there is a catch, and that catch is strong support for the line of reasoning here. Peter believed God before coming to Christ. Can we be certain of this? If we trace how Peter came to Christ in the first chapter of John we find that Andrew, the brother of Peter came to Christ and straightway went and got Peter. We know also that Andrew had been with John the Baptist, so stated in the text. And if Andrew believed God's prophet who prepared the way for Christ, most likely Peter did so too. They both looked for the Messiah (Jn 1:41).

Piper (2000), who is a patron of strict Calvin creed, states that the exchange between Christ and Peter is an example of what God the Father does in the sixth chapter of the Gospel of John. But Piper holds that those given to Christ are simply given, there is no faith needed to be one of the elect. One cannot use this event or this Scripture to show that to be the case. This hermeneutic does not float.

Piper is but taking the lead of Jonathan Edwards (1734) who taught the same in a sermon on Matthew 16:17. But we have

fairly certain signs in the Gospels (Jn 1:35-42) that Peter
believed God at an earlier date. And if this is what Christ meant
in the sixth chapter of John then strict Calvin scholars have the
wrong view. There is a condition to be one of the elect, and then
given to the Son. We must truly believe God, the One Who sent
His Son.

John writes that God will lose no one

During the days of Christ and throughout the years of the
disciples there was often a wide gap of time between believing
God and faith in Christ as the Sent One, the One Who is fully
God and fully man. How do the NT writers deal with this issue?

Further, what was going to guarantee that a true believer in
God would come to faith in Christ? Can God lose some along
the way?

> Jn 6:39-40 -- "This is the will of Him who sent Me,
> that of all that He has given Me I lose nothing, but
> raise it up on the last day. For this is the will of My
> Father, that everyone who beholds the Son and
> believes in Him will have eternal life; and I Myself
> will raise him up on the last day."

According to these two verses all that God has given to
Christ will not be lost. We must ask, "How does God
accomplish this?" We will find out when we get to the Pauline
texts. Suffice for now John says that God gives them to Christ.
And we must understand that those who belonged to God in that
day believed God as Abraham did.

Blinding those who do not believe God

With this distinction in the two faiths let us pursue further
the "faith in God to faith in Christ" option.

Jn 12:37-41 -- "But though He had performed so many signs before them, yet they were not believing in Him. This was to fulfill the word of Isaiah the prophet which he spoke, 'Lord, who has believed our report? And to whom has the arm of the Lord been revealed?' For this reason they could not believe, for Isaiah said again, 'He has blinded their eyes and He hardened their heart, so that they would not see with their eyes and perceive with their heart, and be converted and I heal them.' These things Isaiah said because he saw His glory, and he spoke of Him."

I find it immensely curious that forthwith in the next few verses John tells us that there were still some who believed. Were these people the exception to the claims found in Isaiah? But there is a catch to what Christ says about these new believers.

Jn 12:42-45 -- "Nevertheless many even of the rulers believed in Him, but because of the Pharisees they were not confessing Him, for fear that they would be put out of the synagogue; for they loved the approval of men rather than the approval of God. And Jesus cried out and said, 'He who believes in Me, does not believe in Me, but in Him who sent Me. He who sees Me sees the One who sent me.'"

So who did God blind so that they could not see Christ and be saved? Might they be those who did not believe the One Who sent Christ? Christ was certainly not going to assist those who did not believe God to be saved. Christ was going to be known by only those who truly believe God, for He is One with the Father. His first coming was not the appointed time for all to know Who He was. God still wanted people to live by faith, not by sight.

God blinds people to His written Word and to His Word made flesh, unless people truly believe God. God's Word will mean next to nothing to those people who refuse to believe the author of the Word. Light comes from God.

John indicates in the two linked texts above that the exceptions to the quote from Isaiah are those who do believe in the One Who sent Christ. Christ verifies that they do so; hence they can come to Christ, for God the Father has given them to His Son.

Yes, Christ could have fully revealed Who He was to all. But that was not His purpose at this time. He was going to die for the sins of all in the world, but especially for those who truly believe. If He fully revealed Who He was to all people the cross would have been thwarted, and then no one would be saved.

Is there hope for the lost?

There are many Scriptures all through the NT that speak to this question. But here I want to stay strictly with John. Surely he would have something to say on this subject since belief in Christ is the most prominent theme of what he wrote (Jn 20:31).

What does Christ say to those who do not know the Father or Him? Are they lost without hope?

Jn 7:16b-17 -- "My teaching is not Mine, but His who sent Me. If anyone is willing to do His will, he will know of the teaching whether it is of God or whether I speak from Myself."

Clearly faith in God is not mentioned here, but true belief always means more than a mental nod toward Him. Being willing to do His will would confirm such belief.

And in another place some ask Christ a key question.

Jn 6:28b-29 -- "What shall we do, so that we might work the works of God? Jesus answered and said to them, 'This is the work of God, that you believe in Him whom He has sent.'"

If we refuse to do God's will we certainly are not willing to do His work. But if we will do what God wants we will do the work of God. And His work is to believe in Christ. Needless to say those who put their faith in Christ are doing what God wants them to do. They believe God enough to do what He says which is to put faith in His Son and His work on the cross.

The Words of Christ leave little doubt that the choice to believe God is ours to make. The phrase "If any man is willing" cannot be construed in any other way; the ball is in our court. And if a person believes Him and wants to have a relationship with Him, loves Him, He always gives them to the Son. He has turned all things over to the Son (Mt 11:27; Lk 10:22; Jn 3:31-36, 17:6, 9). And further, God will not be stopped if He knows that someone believes Him. He will send a messenger of His own to get the truth of saving faith in Christ to that person. And His inward testimony to Christ through the Holy Spirit will fully convince them.

On the other hand if a person resists and does not believe God they will have no testimony within them that eternal life is in the Son. In fact they may be blinded until they are willing to fully trust God. They might hear others talk about Christ but they will have no real desire to place their faith in Him.

When we come to these issues later in this book we will address the theological concern for *ordo salutis*, the logical steps required for salvation. For herein lies the crux of the debate between those of Arminius thought and those of Calvin. Is either one correct? Or do we need to reshape our thinking in this area?

The God Who seeks the lost

I am almost certain that strict Calvinists will now say that believing God is caused by and comes from God too. But I know of nothing to base that on in any of the Gospels or the balance of the NT or OT.

Rather in John's Gospel there is more evidence that this is a matter of human choice. Look at these verses, some of which we have reviewed. Read them from the perspective of people doing the choosing.

> Jn 5:24 -- "Truly, truly, I say to you, he who hears My word, and believes Him who sent Me, has eternal life, and does not come into judgment, but has passed out of death into life."

Christ speaks here. If the words of Christ led a person to believe the One Who Sent Him, is this cause and effect? There is influence, of course, but no certainty is stated or implied. We do not find any comparable statement in the Bible that says we cannot believe God unless Christ lets us, or God lets us. But there are plenty of verses that indicate that God knows those who will respond to Him for He knows all things.

And there is yet another text in John that shows how God the Father deals with the lost. We dare not build a case from a single incident, but let's review what Christ said. He speaks to a woman who had some knowledge yet seemingly not enough to make a commitment to God. The woman at the well had some wrinkles in what she thought about God the Father, and Christ responded to her.

> Jn 4:22-24 -- "You worship what you do not know; we worship what we know, for salvation is from the Jews. But an hour is coming, and now is, when the true worshipers will worship the Father in spirit and truth; for such people the Father seeks to be His worshipers. God is spirit, and those who worship Him must worship in spirit and truth."

The key thought for our purpose here is that God the Father "*seeks,*" He does not force, coerce, nor give people to Himself. The verses do not talk about belief, but true faith in God results in worship and love for Him.

We must draw a sharp contrast between a façade of faith, no more than a cerebral nod to truth, as opposed to owning and committing to that truth. God knows those who believe Him and He will accomplish all for them. He gives us Christ: the Lamb of the cross, the Shepherd of His sheep, the Lord of His Church, and the King of His realm.

Prior similar Interpretations of the Gospel of John

There seems to be nothing in print, except in the Scriptures, that speaks to the issue of "faith to faith." L. Vance (1999) comes close in his "The Other Side of Calvinism." C. Olson (2002) does so too in his "Beyond Calvinism and Arminianism." Both of these authors thought that those being handed over by God were the remnant of OT saints.

While I agree in part with Vance and Olson, I also think that John and Paul wrote much more on this subject; and what they wrote leads to a different solution as to who God's elect are. The remnant is but one piece of the puzzle. We must think of the elect as more than the remnant before we can understand all the debated texts on this subject in the NT. A central point to which we must give full weight is that we are born again in Christ by God's will.

Vance and Olson thought that once God the Father gave Christ the remnant of OT saints then everyone has the free will to choose to have faith in Christ. We must find out if the balance of NT Scriptures read in this way. Does Paul say anything on this subject?

Neither of the authors, Vance nor Olson changed their view of the elect. They still held that God's elect are those with faith in Christ, as all defenders of strict free will maintain. Rather I have begun to show that the elect could be a distinct group of people who have yet to believe Christ, but who will do so without fail. These people belong to God by faith. Might these be God's elect who will receive Christ?

Do we need to believe the One Who sent Christ before we can come to faith in Christ? From here on in this book we will pursue the balance of NT Scripture to investigate a "faith to faith" approach. We will see how far this takes us with the most difficult texts in the area of the elect. If you will go further with me you may learn to see the elect in a new way.

John's First Epistle

If you doubt what I have said about some of the texts in the Gospel of John then listen to a person close to the source. The best one to ask, other than God, is the author that wrote the Gospel. What does John say about belief, and faith, and the witness of the Father, in his Epistles?

1 Jn 5:1, 9-12 -- "Whoever believes that Jesus is the Christ is born of God; and whoever loves the Father loves the child born of Him ... If we receive the testimony of men, the testimony of God is greater; for the testimony of God is this, that He has testified concerning His Son. The one who believes in the Son of God has the testimony in himself; the one who does not believe God has made Him a liar, because he has not believed in the testimony that God has given concerning His Son. And the testimony is this, that God has given us eternal life, and this life is in His Son. He who has the Son has the life; he who does not have the Son of God does not have the life."

The underscored text lends more weight to the prior thoughts expressed on the fifth and sixth chapters of the Gospel of John. Here is a brief look at how John sees the logical sequence of salvation. The text moves us further to solid ground under the flag of "faith to faith."

There are two "believes" in this passage. One is to believe in the Son of God. The other is to believe the witness of God that He has given eternal life to us in His Son. The last words are a way of saying to believe God and what He has said. And if we do not believe what God has said about His Son we make God a liar.

We must believe God and His witness about the Son. Those who do not truly believe God will assuredly not listen to His witness to the Son. In fact they may not even have His witness within them. But if we do believe God then He will give us this witness, and we will assuredly believe Christ if we want a relationship with God.

Observe that in this passage we are not born again when we believe God as a witness. We are only born again when we put our faith in His Son. Spiritual birth in the Son comes by believing God and what He says; but the new birth occurs by His Spirit as we put our faith in Christ.

This is a huge part of John's teaching. Those who claim that God chooses to give people to the Son on no grounds except His fiat omit the necessity to believe God and His witness to the Son in the first place. Scripture does not warrant that we detour around God. We cannot have true faith in Christ unless we first believe the One Who sent Him. He is the same One that gives witness to Christ (Mt 3:17; Mk 9:7; Lk 3:22; Jn 5:37; 2 Pt 1:17-18).

Summary of "Faith to Faith" in John's NT Books

Let me add a few more thoughts that may prove significant to those who may question the option of "faith to faith." In order to put our trust in Christ to be saved, do we not need to know that we are lost and a sinner, separated from God? And how do we come to that conclusion unless we first believe God and what He has said?

Can we believe the Lamb of God without, or before, believing the One Who sent the Lamb? That is what both Calvinists and those who espouse total free will in salvation claim, but out of ignorance. Do we really want to think, as the strict Calvinists teach, that God gives people to Christ who do not truly believe Him? This is the fly in their ointment and a big elephant it is.

Today all true Christians accept that we must believe both God the Father and God the Son. But Bible scholars have failed to grasp how the NT writers wrestled with this complex issue in their day. The Scriptures dealing with this problem is at the heart of the debate between those of a Calvin bent and those who say that we have free will to believe.

Now the question arises, does God allow anyone to reach only the "half-way" point, truly to believe God but yet not believe in the One He sent? What prevents this? This issue was very critical at the time of Christ and for the transition period of that day. Is this not important now if we first need to believe God's witness to His Son?

Further there was no NT at that time to explain any of this. So God must do a powerful work to bridge the transition period which was not clearly foreseen in the sacred scrolls. Did God lose some of the OT saints along the way? Will God ever lose some that truly believe Him? We will deal with this problem when we get to Paul's teaching.

There are a few more verses in the Gospel of John that Calvinists use to support their preferred way to look at the Scriptures. I will deal with the balance of these texts when we get to where they fit with what we will discuss. The other passages can be seen in light of what has already been said here.

And likewise we will learn to read the Pauline letters in a way that will challenge our thoughts on the elect, and hence how we view salvation.

Chapter Four

The Early Church Record

Those of high Calvin persuasion who claim that we have no free will have a number of favored proof texts in the book of Acts. A few of these include the following.

Acts 2:46-47 -- "Day by day continuing with one mind in the temple, and breaking bread from house to house, they were taking their meals together with gladness and sincerity of heart, praising God and having favor with all the people. And the Lord was adding to their number day be day those who were being saved."

Acts 8:26-39 -- Philip and the Ethiopian eunuch

Acts 10:1-48 -- Peter and Cornelius

Acts 13:48 -- "And when the Gentiles heard this, they began rejoicing and glorifying the word of the Lord; and as many as had been appointed to eternal life believed."

Acts 16:14 -- "A woman named Lydia, from the city of Thyatira, a seller of purple fabrics, a worshiper of God, was listening; and the Lord opened her heart to respond to the things spoken by Paul."

Acts 18:9-10 -- "And the Lord said to Paul in the night by a vision, "Do not be afraid any longer, but go on speaking and do not be silent; for I am with you, and no man will attack you in order to harm you, for I have many people in this city."

Let's take a walk through the pages of the first years of Church history written by Luke in the book of Acts. Here we catch glimpses of God's work at Pentecost, on Paul's three mission trips and then his defense of the Gospel while under the guard of Rome. As we take the first steps down this path bear in mind the facts from the milieu of that day, those which we reviewed in the second chapter. Are there some who truly believe God out among the scattered in foreign lands? How much evidence will we find in the Book of Acts to weigh in on this premise?

A thorough study of the early days of the Church comes close to confirming, for me, the thoughts that I have shared on the Gospel of John. But you still may hesitate so bear with me for now and then draw your own conclusions.

The book of Acts cuts a slice of history through the years of transition from the nation of Israel to the Church and from OT to NT believer. Hence the words of Luke deserve close scrutiny. We should not try to attain doctrinal certitude from little more than the bare facts of the events that took place. And this would be so no matter how true and precise the record from those days may be. How we perceive the details from this God inspired journal bears much on our dogma; and no less too, our creed will color the way we think about the events of those days.

The traditional way to read the book of Acts presumes the idea that the disciples and Paul took the Good News to those that had never known God. Do the Scriptures bear this out? First, read what Christ said towards the end of His incarnate work.

Jn 10:16 -- "I have other sheep, which are not of this fold; I must bring them also, and they will hear My voice; and they will become one flock with one shepherd."

Then hear what Caiaphas said as high priest under the prompting of God.

Jn 11:51-52 -- "Now he did not say this on his own initiative, but being high priest that year, he prophesied that Jesus was going to die for the nation, and not for the nation only, but in order that He might also gather together into one the children of God who are scattered abroad."

We can take three tacks to explain Christ's claim and the words of the high priest. We might derive the idea, like the Calvinists, that God has a select group out there to whom He will give faith and bring into His flock, both then and for years to come. Or we can take a second path and conclude that since Christ is God, He knows all things. This would include the future and those who would put their trust in Him over the next 2000 plus years. This view would be the one typically held by those with an allegiance to strict free will.

Or third, we might think that both quotes refer to true believers in God around the world at that very time, and of course we cannot omit those who would believe in the future. Note that the one verse alludes to *"the children of God who are scattered."* This phrase is a present tense state of affairs. How do we account for those who might know God at that very time? Should we group them with all unbelievers? Does the Book of Acts even speak to this?

The first interpretation is the only one that would weigh in on the side of "elect then faith." The second could support either "faith then elect" or "faith to faith." The third would be the only view that could account for believers that lived at that same time, but who had yet to learn about Christ. We must stay vigilant so that we let the facts of history speak before we filter them through the grid of our dogma.

Do we dare think that when Peter preached at Pentecost that there were those who knew God among the crowds who came to Jerusalem? Peter made no effort to try to convince them to believe God as Abraham did. That seemed to be a given for many who came. But only those who truly did would claim God's promise (Acts 2:39). And the Lord added to their number day by day those who were being saved (Acts 2:47). Would God save those who did not believe Him by giving them to Christ? Would those who do not believe God answer His call to His Son? I think not.

The context of Peter's sermons does not permit a full analysis of these questions since Peter makes no effort to try and convince people of God. He is talking to at least some that knew God. His aim was to persuade all that believed the promise of God to put their faith in Christ. And surely God acted to save them and add them to the Church. God will not lose any that truly believe Him and His Word.

Are we groundless to think that there were still more who knew God out among the scattered? And had they been given the opportunity to hear about Christ? God would certainly call them too. Paul and others would feel an urgent need to get the Gospel to them, and soon (cf 1 Tm 2:10).

Study the record of the Jerusalem Council and read what Peter says.

> Acts 15:7-9, 11 -- "After there had been much debate, Peter stood up and said to them, 'Brethren, you know that in the early days God made a choice among you, that by my mouth the Gentiles would hear the word of the gospel and believe. And God, who knows the heart, testified to them giving them the Holy Spirit, just as He also did to us; and He made no distinction between us and them, cleansing their hearts by faith. .... But we believe that we are saved through the grace of the Lord Jesus, in the same way as they also are.'"

Of what events did Peter speak? In Acts 10 we find that God chose him to go to Cornelius who lived in Caesarea, a major Roman seaport in Palestine of that day. And who was this Gentile man? To quote Luke, he was a centurion of the Italian cohort, hence a Roman soldier. And he was *"a devout man and one who feared God with all his household, and gave many alms to the Jewish people and prayed to God continually"* (Acts 10:2).

Did this man truly believe and love God? Regardless whether he did or not he still needed to know about Christ to be saved (cf 1 Jn 5:1; Acts 11:14). He certainly seemed to be well acquainted with the Jewish people. Did he believe Moses? For Christ said in John's Gospel, *"If you believed Moses, you would believe Me, for he wrote about Me"* (Jn 5:46). And if perhaps he believed Moses then would he not have known God?

Peter presented the good news of the Gospel and Cornelius came to faith in Christ along with his household. They seem to go from believing God to being cleansed by faith in Christ. God chose them to hear about Christ and be saved; that is very clear from Peter's report to the Council.

Or on the other hand was Cornelius like most monotheistic people who think they worship God, but not really do so? Certainly God came to this man in an amazing and life changing way. God does not do this with most that claim to worship one God. Why is Cornelius so special?

For the view proposed here I do not need to insist that Cornelius was a man of faith in God. But he clearly did things that God asked him to do before he sent for Peter. Thus he showed that he believed at some level; but he did not have the right information to be saved.

Yet, when Peter arrived he did bow to worship Peter, which suggests he lacked full understanding. But does God hold back for what we fail to know, or does He acknowledge true faith? And how many at that time with no written NT understood what God was doing? I wonder how many of us would be saved if we had to have all the details down pat. God sees what is in our heart, and this He knows quite well.

My estimation of this man is that if he had lived prior to Christ then God would have intervened to give Him the promise of the One to come. Thereby he would have been saved in the OT sense. But since Christ had already done the cross work, God, whom He believed (as shown by his actions, though this is never stated in the texts), needed to get the message to him about the One Who had come, the promise now fulfilled. He now needed to know and put his faith in the Son. By God's doing He was born again with faith in Christ.

God went to such incredible lengths to get the Gospel to this man; and this, to me, strongly suggests that he did indeed believe God. And would God choose a Gentile who did not know Him as His example to Peter of what God would do for the Gentiles? Pause to consider the disciples. God chose them to know Christ after they believed God. We saw this in our review of the Gospel of John.

We can speculate with our wildest dreams but we cannot derive set doctrinal boundaries from such events. All that history can show are the facts of that which took place. If the facts happen to fit a doctrine then so be it. But facts dare not contradict doctrine. If they do so then we best take a second look at the doctrine. Needless to say we can always be wrong.

Let's return now to the fifteenth chapter of Acts and the Council in Jerusalem. After the report by Peter, the Lord's half brother, James, adds some brief but thought provoking comments. His words suggest that the Council thought that Paul would go to many cities where he might find others like the man Cornelius. They had been taught the OT and they at least knew of God as described in the OT.

A few may have come to true faith in God. And Paul was to take the good news about Christ to them. James said, *"For Moses from ancient generations has in every city those who preach him, since he is read in the synagogues every Sabbath"* (Acts 15:21). And the disciples had heard Christ say: *"If you believed Moses you would believe Me..."* (Jn 5:46-47).

We must not rush to conclude that none of the people in those distant places of worship and study were children of God at that very hour. Most would have heard of His promise of One to come. And from what we know, the Scriptures of that day were in the language of the common people. The Word would have been easy to read and grasp by most of the Gentiles where Paul went on his travels.

Was this part of God's plan for Paul? Perhaps this was one reason that Paul could spend just a few short days in a city and get permanent results. The Word of God and the witness of the Holy Spirit can do great wonders in those lives that are prepared.

Not all OT believers lived in Israel. Luke tells of Philip who was led by the Spirit to a chariot in the desert (Acts 8). And there he met the Ethiopian eunuch who had gone to worship in

Jerusalem. While on his journey home this member of the Queen's court and guardian of the Queen's wealth sat and read from the book of Isaiah.

He surely believed what was written in the Sacred Scrolls of that day but did not grasp whom the passage talked about. Need we ask why God sent Philip to this man? He accepts Christ on the spot. Here again, is a strong prospect for "faith to faith." God went to astounding lengths to reach those who knew Him. And He will always do so when someone is ready.

As Paul and his friends went from city to city they left no synagogue or place of prayer untouched. That was where they would find those who might know God, prepared by the Spirit for the good news about Christ. And Luke affirms that Paul often reasoned with Jews, proselytes, and the devout.

And we should not forget those Gentiles who feared God. Sometimes there were just a few; a few times there were many. And when Paul and his troupe came to Thessalonica (Acts 17) they were greeted by a "great multitude" of God-fearers in the synagogue; those taught from the Word of the OT in a language they could understand, Greek. For Luke says that they were Greeks.

The book of Acts does not even say that these Gentiles believed. Rather Luke writes that a few of the Jews were persuaded and joined Paul and Silas along with some women and those who feared God. If some had believed God before, how would they have known about Christ prior to Paul's arrival?

We can declare without the slightest reservation that several years after Christ left this earth there were still those in distant lands who did not know that He had lived, died, and rose again. And beyond doubt, at least a few were true believers. I can say this without the least bit of hesitation and you would agree with me. You might ask, how could I claim this? And if you did not ask, you should have.

Let's go with Paul to Ephesus on his third mission trip (Acts 19). There we would have trekked with him through the upper country, somewhat off the beaten path. This was years after Christ's ascension; and we would have found some men who were still looking for the Messiah. They were twelve disciples of John the Baptist, and Paul informed them that Christ had indeed come. This was great news for them; all twelve, 100 percent, were baptized in the name of Christ.

They had heard the witness of the last OT prophet who had told them of the Lamb of God Who was to come (Jn 1:6-8). And if they heeded his prophetic word then they knew God too. We gained this insight from the Gospel of John and his report on the witnesses to Christ: Moses, the Word, John the Baptist, God the Father, and the works of Christ. A wealth of evidence says that these men believed God before Paul came.

These twelve men give us the courtroom proof that would convince any jury that there were those who had genuine faith in God out in the distant regions, years after the main events of Christ's life in the land of promise. Does our doctrine on salvation need to take into account people such as this? If so, how do we explain them? Do we have a basis for knowing why every last one of them accepts Christ? None were lost.

When we read the NT we are all too quick to dismiss the work of God beyond the land of Palestine in that day. But whom do we find coming to see Christ in the twelfth chapter of John? They were Greeks from another country and they were on their way to worship at the feast in Jerusalem. They too, were drawn to Jesus, and what did they search for? And shortly Christ said, *"And I, if I am lifted up from the earth, will draw all men to Myself"* (Jn 12:32).

Paul did reach out to the raw Gentile world in a few places. In Athens he spoke at Mars Hill with a message about the unknown God, and then he spoke of Christ. The message he gave in that place was a marked contrast to what he spoke in the synagogue. (Compare Acts 13:16-41 with Acts 17:22-34).

In the meeting place of the Jews he quoted the OT at length, at the Areopagus much less so. But the message in both places implied that people must believe God as well as accept His Son. Paul seemed to teach about God the Father to draw people to the Son. Paul seemed to aim God-inspired reasoning toward "faith to faith."

Now go to Acts 13:48. *"...As many as had been appointed to eternal life believed."* On the surface this quote reads like the strict Calvin scholars are right. The text for them is certain proof for "elect then faith." The word sequence says that they were appointed to eternal life before they believed.

On the other hand, Luke and Paul may have had good reason to think that some in that city already knew God. They then believed in the Son of God. Paul as a Jewish scholar would have known that their Scrolls, their only Scriptures, said that Abraham believed God. Now how does Paul persuade the people to believe the Good News about Christ?

Be careful to study the full text of what happened (Acts 13:14-52). Luke says that Paul first went to the synagogue and spoke to the *"Men of Israel, and you who fear God."* In his message Paul did not try to persuade them about God, but rather he seems to assume that they know God. He reviews a number of things that God did in the OT and then goes on to talk about John the Baptist. Then Paul presents Christ.

Luke describes the response of the people in Acts 13:42-44. They *"begged"* for more to be taught the next Sabbath. This is a fairly dramatic reaction to a brief message from a stranger that has come to town for a few days. Most likely some of them had the witness of God within them (1 Jn 5:9-10). So *"Many of the Jews and of the God-fearing proselytes followed Paul and Barnabas."* The next week nearly the whole city gathered to hear the Word. Luke says most of the Jews turned against Paul; but quite a few of the Gentiles believed.

The whole city seemed to have had some idea about God; they were excited and wanted to hear more of what Paul had to say. I think the circumstances of what took place, with their fervent embrace of Christ, favors the thought that many belonged to God in the OT sense. The good news from Paul won their quick acclaim. And if some were true believers of God before, then He would have appointed them to eternal life (cf Jn 5:24), even before Paul came.

We will never know enough about the facts of such events to build a case for doctrinal certainty. And it could be that Paul didn't even know the status of their hearts before. Perhaps in his speech, they at that time came to believe God and the Sent One. We just need to be careful not to conclude too much from these cases since "faith to faith" is a viable option. We should not simply take for granted that none of the people knew or had learned from God before (Jn 6:45).

No matter, they still needed to hear that God sent His Son to die on the cross in their place, and that He now lives. They still needed to believe in Him, the promise now fulfilled by God, for they had yet to hear of Christ's death and resurrection. The most that they could have been in the OT sense is reckoned as righteous due to believing God and His promise of One to come. But Paul told them about God's Gospel that had come to pass. And I think Paul meant what he said when he addressed the Gentiles in the synagogue as *"you who fear God"* (Acts 13:16). Of course not all did, nor did they all believe.

I am less convinced of the strict Calvin view on the above verse when we return to the summary report of the Council in Jerusalem (Acts 15). Paul begins with the God of the OT to persuade these people to accept Christ. Do they not need to believe the OT Word in order to accept Christ? And if they trust what was said in the OT, they have learned from God. The evidence in this passage that faith follows election is weak. To me, the better thought is that "faith in Christ follows true faith in God." These are the people who pursue by belief; God had appointed them to life before since they believed Him. They will most certainly believe in Christ.

Consider Lydia (Acts16:14). She heeds the Gospel message. But what else does Luke say? She was *"a worshiper of God,"* at the time Paul gave her the good news. Here is irresistible grace in action; but most likely the pattern is "faith to faith." In fact when you study the full text, Luke does not even mention faith or belief on Lydia's part, just as he didn't in Thessalonica (Acts 17:1-9). The only thing that Luke writes is that God opened her heart. She seemed to know and believe God already and just needed to hear about Christ.

If we had read about Lydia in a book of the OT, we would have been fairly certain that she would have been included under the umbrella of belief. And of course in those days they had nothing but the OT. God opened her heart to His Son, and this confirms for me that she knew God, before Paul spoke to her. Then she asked Paul if he counted her faithful. What would that have meant if she were just a new believer?

I find the doctrine of irresistible grace as taught by Calvin scholars highly suspect based on the scant details from such events in the book of Acts. No doubt God's Spirit will fully convince a person to come to Christ when one truly believes God.

Now let's compare what Luke reports about a second convert in the same city. Review the events of the night spent in jail at Philippi. This is a very intriguing case. Here we do find faith, and this faith isn't just in Christ. Read the full text (Acts 16:22-34). So much is made of verse 31, but verse 34 also adds a smidgen of insight. Let's read the text beginning at verse 29:

Acts 16:29-34 -- "And he called for lights and rushed in, and trembling with fear he fell down before Paul and Silas, and after he brought them out, he said, "Sirs, what must I do to be saved?" They said, "Believe in the Lord Jesus, and you shall be saved, you and your household." And they spoke the word of the Lord to him together with all who were in his house. And he took them that very hour of the night and washed their wounds, and immediately he was baptized, he and all his household. And he brought them into his house and set food before them, and rejoiced greatly, having believed in God with his whole household."

What did Paul tell the jailer, for this is the key to the whole passage? *"Believe on the Lord Jesus and you shall be saved..."* Here is a promise. This is God's testimony to what happens when we believe in His Son (cf 1 Jn 5:10).

This is the Gospel of God. So if we refuse to believe this testimony, which is to refuse to believe God, we will not come to faith in Christ. But if we do believe what God says and want to have a relationship with Him, then we will trust Christ.

After the initial call to believe in Christ then Paul and Silas spoke the word of the Lord to the jailer, and those of his house. Luke then writes that the man believed God, not just the Son of God. Does this not mean that Paul taught him about God the Father as well as God the Son, and most likely the Holy Spirit too?

Granted, these facts alone do not lead to any firm conclusion, but the record speaks of more than just faith in Christ. Here was a man who definitely had no prior relationship with God, and no faith in Christ. Luke's report is striking. This is one of the few times in Acts where he records that the person believed God. Most of the time Luke writes about faith in Christ, or the Lord, or just believing. And then there are a few times when belief is not mentioned at all.

Now I ask, "Why does Luke mention belief in God with this man and there is not the slightest mention of any kind of belief with Lydia?" They are both from the same city. Could we make a case that belief for some people is not required, tongue in cheek of course? We dare not argue from silence, as this is fatal to any worthwhile debate. None the less the details of situations like these can suggest a pattern.

A still more convincing case of "faith to faith" in Acts is the outreach in Berea (Acts 17:10-12). There the people search the Scriptures to verify what Paul told them. And there were Greeks in this city too, in all likelihood reading the Word in their own language. I think we can safely say that they believed what had been written. Why else would they go to and search through the Scriptures so quickly? We have by now seen that if they believed Moses they would believe in Christ. And I'm sure they also knew what the other OT prophets had foretold.

Before we leave Acts, let's pause for a brief visit in Corinth (Acts 18). First we find Paul at the synagogue reasoning with the Jews and the Greeks. The Jews resist the message and Paul leaves the synagogue and goes to a house next door. There he finds a man called *"Titius Justus, a worshiper of God"*. And then, too, Luke says in verse 18:8 that Crispus, the head of the synagogue, believed in the Lord with his entire household. Later we find that many in Corinth believed.

Then the Lord tells Paul to keep on speaking *"for I have many people in this city."* These words do not refer to the future. No doubt there were more people like Titius Justus and Crispis. Compare these words with what Christ said in John 10:16 and what Caiaphas, the high priest, said in John 11:51-52.

Without question raw Gentiles came to the Lord in Corinth, not just God-fearers, proselytes, and Jews. I would expect that many would turn to God through the witness of those who came to know Christ. But I also think, from what Luke writes, that there were those people who knew God at that very hour when the Lord told Paul to keep on speaking. They needed the Gospel message.

They were part of the transition that was taking place. They were not some esoteric people who did not know God yet. God will spare no means to reach those with but meager true faith in Him. He will lose no one. Of course we can interpret the same passage in terms of God knowing all things, but that is not as persuasive.

Summary of the Book of Acts

From this brief study of Acts we can see that the doctrine we hold to will shape how we interpret the bare facts of history. Most who are honest in their study and search acknowledge this. We just need to be cautious and not stretch what we claim beyond the limits of the Word. I readily admit that I could be wrong on these texts. I do not think I am, but there are others who would think otherwise, and so maybe the reasoning here could be full of holes. Nonetheless, as you can see, there is often more than one way to look at the same events.

When I think back to the book of Jeremiah in the OT we find a group of people in Egypt who held to their own slant on history (Jer 44:15-19). They would not listen to their prophet and they lost all hope of salvation.

Fortunately we are not dealing with that kind of twisted thinking here. If we see things from a slightly different angle so be it. But let's not make our point of view a litmus test for what is truth as long as the basics are in place. In the end we could all be wrong on some of these issues.

At this point in our search, let's take our leave from the book of Acts. But we will check back for more observations as we delve into some of the letters that Paul wrote.

Chapter Five

Letters to Churches

Galatians

Most scholars of the Word regard Paul's letter to the churches of Galatia as his first of record. So here we have some of his earliest thoughts, and faith is the bedrock for the main theme of what he writes in this epistle.

Paul explains how we need to live by faith after we put our trust in Christ, not going back to the law of the OT as taught by the Judaizers. Yet, what Paul says about faith and salvation is quite compelling for the thesis of this book. We need to look closely at what he tells us about the faith of an OT patriarch.

Gal 3:5-9 -- "So then, does He who provides you with the Spirit and works miracles among you, do it by the works of the Law, or by hearing with faith? Even so

Abraham believed God, and it was reckoned to him as righteousness. Therefore, be sure that it is those who are of faith who are sons of Abraham. The Scripture, foreseeing, that God would justify the Gentiles by faith, preached the gospel beforehand to Abraham, saying, 'All the nations will be blessed in you.' So then those who are of faith are blessed with Abraham, the believer."

Abraham believed God Who gave him the promise (Gn 15:1-6). All nations would be blessed in him at some appointed time yet future. One would come from his lineage; and we know that this One was none other than Christ.

A little later Paul's remarks go on to say:

Gal 3:22-26 -- "But the Scripture has shut up everyone under sin, so that the promise by faith in Jesus Christ might be given to those who believe. But before faith came, we were kept in custody under the law, being shut up to the faith which was later to be revealed. Therefore the Law has become our tutor to lead us to Christ, so that we may be justified by faith. But now that faith has come, we are no longer under a tutor. For you are all sons of God through faith in Christ Jesus."

Paul writes that faith in Christ was "shut up" in the OT; such faith was not made known before the days of incarnation. Most OT saints knew little more from the prophets than faint impressions here and there of what was to come. And Paul wrote a few other times about the veiled nature of this faith in the Son of God. (Rom 16:25; 1 Cor 2:7-8; Eph 3:3-11; Col 1:25-27, 2:2).

But didn't Abraham believe? Didn't all OT saints believe and it was reckoned to them as righteousness? Yes, but OT saints believed God, and He gave them the promise of One to come. They claimed the promise because they believed the One that made the promise.

With the belief of Abraham in mind, observe what Paul says in the text above; the *promise by faith in Jesus Christ is given to those who believe*. The question I ask about this statement by Paul is to what or to whom does the verb "believe" link? If God made the promise and is also the One Who gives then I think the word "believe" would refer to God. The believers are those who receive the gift of the promise that is by faith in Christ. Just like OT saints who believed God, NT saints believe God and are given the promise, but now the promise fulfilled rather than the promise that was yet to come.

This may well be the best way to read the text. The concept of "faith to faith" seems key to what takes place. Without this concept the wording is awkward. Greek language buffs may be able to convince me that the verb "believe" in this context refers to Christ alone, but I need to see the evidence; more so since the verb is either continuous or repeated action in the Koinè Greek.

The text is powerful when read in the way suggested, granted that this fits with the Greek wording. We just need to bear in mind the huge influence that the OT had on those who first read Paul's letters; to believe God as Abraham did is more apt to have been their mindset.

The only Scripture known to them was the Sacred Scrolls of the OT; what Paul sent to them was not yet seen as part of Scripture. Hence, when the verb "believe" stands alone, with no clear and direct link to Christ, we must weigh the option of whether Paul is talking about believing God. And this premise passes the litmus of context; Paul had just written about the patriarch who had learned from God.

If I should learn that these thoughts on the text fail to hold up under the scrutiny of scholars of the Greek language, then so be it. A tint of error in this section of our study would not tarnish the premise of "faith to faith." But since we have seen that the concept is active in a few other places this may help us gain some insight into the above text too.

1 and 2 Thessalonians

Let's now look at two more early letters by Paul, those sent to the young church in Thessalonica. Here we find his first written thoughts on the theme of God's "choice." But keep in mind the events of that day; we must distill some of the facts that we have from the historical record compiled by Luke in the book of Acts (cf Acts 17:1-4).

Luke sketches the details of Paul's first contact with the synagogue of that city. His account favors the thought that a few, if not many, knew God before Paul came. Luke attests to *"a large number"* of those who feared God in the synagogue; and many seem to have been prepared to accept the message of Paul as soon as they heard it. They were convinced of Christ in an incredible short span of time. Such a brief stay, three weeks, has all the marks of God doing a mighty work in some of their lives before Paul came.

And more, from the Acts record, Paul seemed to make no attempt to persuade them about God; he spoke only of Christ. Compare this to his address at Mars Hill or his work with the jailer at Philippi. Paul seemed to assume that some believed God; and why shouldn't he if they had been taught out of the OT in their native language? He found them in the synagogue; this is where he would find those who might truly believe God.

Paul wrote in his letter to the church there:

1 Thes 1:2-5a -- "We give thanks to God always for all of you making mention of you in our prayers; constantly bearing in mind your work of faith and labor

of love and steadfastness of hope in our Lord Jesus Christ in the presence of our God and Father, knowing, brethren beloved by God, His choice of you; for our gospel did not come to you in word only, but also in power and in the Holy Spirit and with full conviction..."

What does Paul mean by *"choice"* here? The word precedes the mention of the Gospel. I think that the best explanation is that some, if not many, believed God before Paul came and, of course, God would indeed choose them for salvation, to be in Christ. God knew those that belonged to Him. Those that did not have true faith would not be so chosen. And there were probably many that would fall on that side of the line, not being of genuine faith.

Luke also tells us about a mob that sent the city into an uproar at the end of Paul's three-week stay (Acts 17:5-7). There was a huge split in the crowd at the synagogue. With the near riot that fired up the crowd, how do these new Christians explain that some come to Christ while most of their best friends not do so? One reason Paul may have used the word *"choice,"* perhaps, is to speak to this question.

But more likely the word told them they were secure in God. Paul wanted to make clear that God gave them to Christ; God willed for them to accept the Gospel. In fact God made the choice to have them put their faith in His Son. He handed them over to the Son. Their belief in God was genuine, while those that did not accept Christ lacked true faith in God and were not so chosen. Might Paul reason this way?

There is nothing written in either the letter to the church, nor in the book of Acts that gives any hint that these people had never believed God before. In fact the evidence is to the contrary. A *"large number"* had given up their idols. Would none of them have had true faith in the living God?

What message would Paul have sent to these people if he had told them they had never really believed or loved God before? Some would have believed Moses since they were found in the synagogue. They had the OT in their own language. Most likely that was why there were so many Gentiles; and Luke says they were Greeks (Acts 17:4).

Paul says further:

1 Thes 1:8-10 – "For the word of the Lord has sounded forth from you, not only in Macedonia and Achaia, but also in every place your faith toward God has gone forth, so that we have no need to say anything. For they themselves report about us what kind of a reception we had with you, and how you turned to God from idols to serve a living and true God, and to wait for His Son from heaven, whom He raised from the dead, that is Jesus, who rescues us from the wrath to come."

Note the sequence of these words; the people turned to God to wait for His Son. This is now a familiar flow of thought and once again appears to be "from God to Christ." God chose those who believed Him to be in Christ. We know the Epistles are penned with God's breath through the mind and hand of Paul. And we must yield to the words he used and the sequence of those words.

By Luke's account in Acts of what happened during those days, the Gentiles who feared God had no doubt turned from idols before Paul ever came on the scene. But if they did not turn to God until Paul came, most likely the sequence of events would have been much the same. This is the stream of thought that Paul spells out.

The time gap between true belief in God and faith in Christ may have been short, much shorter, perhaps almost in the same instant. But I think the logical flow of belief would have been identical. The habit of Paul is to present God as seen in the OT and then he leads the people to the Sent One.

Most students of the Word ask more searching questions about a text in Paul's second letter to these same people.

> 2 Thes 2:13b-14 – "But we should always give thanks to God for you, brethren beloved by the Lord, because God has chosen you from the beginning for salvation through sanctification by the Spirit and faith in the truth. It was for this He called you through our gospel, that you may gain the glory of our Lord Jesus Christ."

We know that these verses say that God chose them for salvation from the beginning. But what does Paul mean? If they believed God before Paul arrived then this might support the idea of "faith to faith." If God chose them by fiat, with no prior condition of faith in Him, then this would support the view of "elect then faith." If God acted, simply knowing that they would respond to the Gospel message, then one might argue for "faith then elect." Which way should we go?

Three solid reasons compel me to lean toward "faith to faith" as the best fit. First, Luke writes that there was a great multitude of those who feared God; and they heard and followed Paul. These were the first NT believers in that place. And Paul's wording in the first chapter of his first letter to that church adheres to this sequence (1 Thes 1:8-10).

Second, Luke's record in Acts states that Paul only taught there for three Sabbaths (Acts 17:2). And his work was done in the synagogue, the only place that Luke mentions. Paul did not appear to be out to convert those who worshipped false gods at that time. Luke does not cite such an outreach in the Acts account; but in Paul's letter to the church, if read alone, we might wrongly assume that to be the case.

If they had been under the influence of idols when Paul first went there he would not have found the God-fearing Gentiles with the Jews. And to take that many from false gods to faith in Christ seems a bit of a stretch for such a brief visit. Most strangers that come to a town do not have that much pull. Still, the Philippian jailer did respond quickly, so there is precedent.

And third we know that Paul reasoned with people from the Scriptures. The Word of the OT is all Paul had plus the good news about Christ. Paul seemed to work from the base that some of the people there truly believed God. From that base God calls them through His Gospel to gain the glory of Christ. I think Paul declared that God chose them, because they had true faith in Him. Might we conclude that God chooses all that have true faith in Him to have the riches in and of Christ?

Paul states too that salvation came through *"sanctification by the Spirit and faith in the truth."* So the Spirit had a role and *"faith in the truth"* played a part. And the order of words chosen by Paul suggests that the Spirit and belief in the truth were operative in their lives prior to the Gospel call. Might they have been prepared for the message? Did they not already believe God and His Word?

But there is no salvation without Christ. So God the Father called those at Thessalonica through the Gospel to be saved and to gain the glory of Christ. I am close to being sold that for those who received this letter the path to saving faith began by believing God. But how would they gain Christ unless God made that happen? Unless God chose them He could have lost some that belonged to Him.

The word *"beginning"* in 1 Thes 2:13 should arouse our sense of chronology or stream of events. The word surely speaks to a date before Paul came on the scene. That leaves us with two possible dates.

The word could refer to when the people first believed God, before Paul came. Or the point in time could have been at the pre-dawn of creation. The context seems to imply the former since Paul writes about sanctification and faith in the truth which both seem to have been active prior to the Gospel call. But which beginning Paul means does not make one speck of a difference. Both would be true.

Now, we can insist that the action of God is by His arbitrary fiat, with no prior belief; but an equally strong exegesis does not take that route. All we must do is include the record from the book of Acts to see the second option. But those who received the letter from Paul would not have any need to read the account by Luke; they knew whether they had truly believed God before Paul came on the scene.

1 and 2 Corinthians

The first three chapters of Paul's letter to the church at Corinth yields a fertile field for those who teach strict Calvinism. Some of the key passages are:
----

1 Cor 1:9 -- "God is faithful through whom you were called into fellowship with His Son, Jesus Christ our Lord."

1 Cor 1:23-31 – "But we preach Christ crucified, to Jews a stumbling block and to Gentiles foolishness, but to those who are the called, both Jews and Greeks, Christ the power of God and the wisdom of God. Because the foolishness of God is wiser than men, and the weakness of God is stronger than men. For consider your calling, brethren, that there were not many wise according to the flesh, not many mighty, not many noble; but God has chosen the foolish things of the world to shame the wise, and God has chosen the weak things of the world to shame the things which are strong, and the base things of the world and

the despised, God has chosen, the things that are not, so that He may nullify the things that are, so that no man may boast before God. But by His doing you are in Christ Jesus, who became to us wisdom from God, and righteousness and sanctification, and redemption, so that, just as it is written. 'Let him who boasts, boast in the Lord.'"

Paul writes that God does many things in these verses, for those whom He does them for and to. Of course, Paul is talking to those in the Church of God, which is at Corinth (1 Cor 1:2), those who are set apart in Christ. Hence, the people that Paul addresses are those who believe. But what do they believe?

1 Cor 1:21 -- "For since in the wisdom of God the world through its wisdom did not come to know God, God was well-pleased through the foolishness of the message preached to save those who believe."

If we restrict the verb "believe" in this verse to link to Christ only, and omit that we need to believe God too, then all that Paul writes in these three chapters are rife with the full rule of God. He indeed is sovereign in all the actions that take place here. Paul even says that no man can boast since we are in Christ by God's doing (1 Cor 1:30-31). Not one thing man has done (1 Cor 1:26) in his wisdom, strength, or rank in life has achieved the fact that we are in Christ. Rather through the message preached God saved those that believed.

And what was the message preached? If we read the first verse of First Corinthians, chapter two, in the right way, the message preached was the *"testimony of God."* So did the people believe what God said? And if they did, did they not believe God, for His testimony is His witness about the Son. I question here if we should restrict the verb "believe" of verse twenty-one to Christ alone, since the action once again is continuous or repeated.

We find out more about the message preached by Paul in chapter two. The message was God's wisdom, which had been hidden from Man but known by God before the ages (1 Cor 2:7-8). Why did God keep it from being known? Because if those in the day of Christ had understood they would not have crucified the Lord; and as a result no one would be saved.

Then Paul quotes in part an OT passage from Isaiah (Is 64:4) about the wonderful and magnificent things that God has in store for those who love Him. What are these things that He has in store for us, those that truly believe Him shown in our love for Him? Isn't what He has done for us in Christ part of what He does for those who believe and love Him?

> 1 Cor 2:9 -- "But just as it is written, 'Things which eye has not seen and ear has not heard, and which have not entered the heart of man, all that God has prepared for those who love Him.'"

At this time I will not say more about those that love God, but we will see this same exact phrase again in much the same type of discussion by Paul in the eighth chapter of Romans. There we get a clearer picture of what Paul is saying.

One more quick note, before we leave this letter, we need to pause and consider what the city of Corinth was like. The city was famed for false gods among the pagans, and for the varied Greek philosophy taught there. I doubt that anyone in God's Church thought that Paul was saying that God gives or does anything for those who did not believe and love God. He does the things written about here for His own, those that truly believe God. I do not think God does these things for those who will not hear His message. And they need to hear and believe His message before they can or will come to faith in Christ.

In these verses Paul does not say one word that claims that God causes people to believe or love Him. Rather Paul drives the point home that all are welcome. God favors no person and works mostly with those who do not measure up to the world's sense of worth. Wealth, a bright mind, power, the wisdom of man, and rank or status make no difference to God. All can come who will believe the foolishness of the message preached. Those with misplaced values and inflated pride are the least likely to listen and believe what God has said.

The saints at Corinth were still caught in the grips of the world's measure of worth, one notch better than thou. They were immature in their walk with the Lord and they chose up sides, splitting the church due to corrupt values. And Paul tells them that God did not choose anyone for salvation based on a standard found in the world. In fact such corrupt values get in the way of belief in what appears to be a foolish message. Yes, we who believe God's Word will accept Christ and serve Him. As Paul says in his letter (1 Cor 2:16), we know these things because we have the mind of Christ.

Last of all; let's go to the final three verses of chapter three.

1 Cor 3:21-23 -- "So then let no one boast in men. For all things belong to you, whether Paul or Apollos or Cephas or the world or life or death or things present or things to come; all things belong to you, and you belong to Christ; and Christ belongs to God."

Philippians

A brief look at Paul's letter to the Church at Phillipi is worth the time and effort for our study.

From the book of Acts we know just a few things about Paul's work in this city (cf Acts 16:12-40). He spent time on the beach at a prayer meeting, then in a jail, then in the house of the jailer, and later at the home of Lydia. There was no place of worship for the Jews in the city. Those who turned to Christ, which we know about, were Lydia and the jailer with his family.

From what Luke reports we find that Lydia worshiped God, and He opened her heart to the message of Paul (Acts 16:14). In contrast the jailer clearly did not know God at all; Luke made the point that this was new to him (Acts 16:34) when He wrote that the jailer believed God.

Now go to a verse that those of Calvin persuasion often use.

Phil 1:29 -- "For to you it has been granted for Christ's sake, not only to believe in Him, but also to suffer for His sake."

This sounds like sure-fire teaching on God permitting them to believe in Christ. And the verse just before states that salvation is from God, further adding to this point of view. So God is active in granting and giving salvation.

But this again is not the full story in this letter from Paul. Go to Philippians 3:9. I do not like to start in the middle of a paragraph, but here goes:

Phil 3:9 -- "...and may be found in Him, not having a righteousness of my own derived from the Law, but that which is through faith in Christ, the righteousness which comes from God on the basis of faith..."

The flow of words in this text leans strongly in the direction of "faith to faith." Do the two words translated *"faith"* refer precisely to the same thing? If so, then why repeat? Why not stop with *"...through faith in Christ"* and not add the last part of the sentence? Is the last phrase redundant? Might not the first word (*faith*) mean faith in Christ and the second word (*faith*) refer to faith in God? If so, then we cannot contest this sequence of "faith to faith." We must remember that to the people of that day, if they had faith they would think they still needed to believe God not just the second person of the Trinity.

Putting the two passages together, it seems likely that God grants people to have faith in Christ if and only if they believe God, the One Who sent Him. Hence, the elect are most likely those that believe God.

I would not want to build a case on this passage alone, but the pattern has been set. As the evidence begins to mount there seems to be a pattern that we need to heed.

Let's now go to Ephesians and Romans. I hope the study of these epistles will clear up, and not muddy the waters, difficult texts as they may be.

Ephesians

Context, context, context must rule the day when we strive to get to the true meaning of God's Word. Language, grammar, themes, and such are to be studied. But we must also pay due heed to the impact of the time and place of the author and reader of that day.

By Luke's report (Acts 18:18ff), Paul arrived in the city of Ephesus toward the last days of his second mission trip; he was accompanied by a husband and wife team, Priscilla and Aquila. As was Paul's custom he first went to the known meeting place of the Jews and tried to reach them for Christ. He only spent a brief few days there, as he needed to return to his home church in Antioch. The Jews asked him to stay, but he refused. He gave them his word that he would return at a later time, Lord willing.

A short while after Paul's departure a man by the name of Apollos came to the city. He was from Egypt by birth, and sometime before he had known and followed John the Baptist.

He was a gifted speaker and quite persuasive. But his message was deficient in some way, as he did not have a full grasp of what he needed to teach. Hence, Priscilla and Aquila, having learned from Paul, showed him more about the *"way of God."* Later this servant of God left to take the Gospel to other places, ending up in Corinth (1 Cor 1:12).

True to his promise Paul soon returned to Ephesus. We then gain a more complete picture of some of the people who were being reached with the Gospel (cf Acts 18-19). Paul found a group of twelve men who had also been disciples of John the Baptist. The text suggests that these men may not have been in the city proper, since Paul passed through what Luke called the *"upper country."* These men had yet to hear that Christ had come. Paul baptized them into Christ, all of them.

As was pointed out before, the fact that we find these men, at this time and place, adds more weight to the growing evidence for the approach offered in this book. All good Bible scholars would agree that these men had faith in God before Paul met them; and years had passed since the ascension of Christ. Paul had completed two mission trips by then, and he was on his third. Where Paul found them attests to the reach of John the Baptist. They like Apollos had been taught by a prophet in Israel who came before Christ. And these men were out there among the scattered. They believed God, and they knew the Messiah was to come, but they knew nothing about the Holy Spirit.

And if these men believed God, He would give them to Christ; and they would believe in the Son of God for salvation. They were appointed to eternal life before Paul met them (cf Jn 5:24). Such men make the case for irresistible grace in the strict Calvin sense highly suspect. Still, we can surely say that God gives His grace in Christ to those that believe God.

Then Paul went again to teach in the synagogue, and he did so for about three months. He reasons with all those who would listen about the Kingdom of God. The Jews did not chase him out quickly and there seems to have been some who responded to the Gospel.

Did any of the others from the crowd at the synagogue know God before Paul came? There is no way that we can be certain. But once again, we do know what Christ said. If they believed Moses then they would believe Him (Jn 5:46-47).

Luke writes that towards the end of three months some in the synagogue became hardened and were speaking evil of them. Most rejected Christ. So Paul moves his work, taking the believers with him, to the school of Tyrannus, where he taught daily for about two more years. All who lived in the area of Ephesus heard the Word of the Lord, both Jews and Greeks.

To sum up, the Gospel message reached a mixed group in that city. I have few reservations about saying that they range from believers in God before Paul came, to the most pagan. I'm sure that there were those of the Jews who had no true belief in God before, had been quite devoted to Law, and then learned from Paul about faith. But like the twelve that had followed the prophet John, I think there were also some among them who did know God. The fact that Paul taught them for three months before strife arose tells us that there must have been some that were prepared for the Gospel message, and that this was so from the start of his work in that place.

Just as important for the context of that day is to consider what Scriptures they used in that early church. Luke describes Apollos as skilled in the OT. Likewise Paul used the OT to persuade effectively. The Jews had the Word in Hebrew and the Greeks had the Scrolls in the Greek language, much more potent when read in one's native tongue. Most of all, there was no NT, at least none that they would have seen as God's Word. This strengthens the reasoning here.

Those that taught started with God as depicted in the OT. They taught about faith, believing God as Abraham did. This would have been the most aphoristic given for all in that day. Paul of course would draw a sharp line between living by faith, as opposed to living by the Law.

But he also needed to persuade those who truly believed God to put their faith in Christ. And I doubt that he can argue that point unless he makes the last faith conditional on the first. If he doesn't, Paul would have been seen as teaching idol worship to the Jews. And he wouldn't have made much sense to the Greeks who had heard of Abraham who believed God.

If I dare put myself in their place I would have thought that belief would start with God the Father, just like their Sacred Scrolls said. And why would they believe God with us if they didn't believe God in the first place? This idea is sanctioned most by their high regard for the only Scriptures they knew. And Paul's letters to the saints in Galatia and Rome show that the foundation for what he taught began with Abraham, and He believed the One Who sent Christ.

But we do not find this basic teaching in Paul's letter to the church at Ephesus. Why not?

The church at Ephesus had come of age by the time they received their letter from Paul. They had been taught more doctrine and essentials of the faith than any other church to whom Paul wrote. Apollos spent time there. Priscilla and Aquila were there. Paul went there twice and the second time he spent about two and a half years developing the people in the faith. And they had twelve disciples of John the Baptist who had spent time there. The church had a wealth of instruction in the Lord.

All the teachers would have taught from the OT. The people had also heard at length what God was doing in and through Christ. When Paul wrote his letter he sent it to a relatively mature church body, those who were God's people, those who were solid believers. I do not think Paul had any need to strengthen their need to believe God. That would have been a core axiom to them, one that they would never pause to question in the slightest.

Rather Paul's purpose was to put the grandeur of Christ on display and to explain and exalt God's plan to sum up all things in Christ (Eph 1:10). Working toward this end Paul shows how we as the Church fit into God's plan. We are the body of Christ on earth.

With this brief review of the attendant circumstances of that day, we can now try to think through how we might have read Paul's letter. Dare we read his Epistle as we walk in the footsteps of someone that first believed God and later accepted Christ? Dare we read as one who only had the OT for their Scriptures? Would this shape how we would have come to terms with what Paul wrote?

The letter might, in fact, be easier to read from this point of view. The context framed by time, place, person, and the known Scripture of that day, is a must for an honest and thorough study of what Paul says. And for the subject at hand these may be critical.

Through the lens of this background, let's now examine what Paul tells the church body in that place. Since NT doctrine was still somewhat new for them they most likely would have made a greater distinction in the Godhead than what we might today. (We still need to do so in the area of function or role.) Paul says:

> Eph 1:2-4a -- "Grace to you and peace from God our Father and the Lord Jesus Christ. Blessed be the God and Father of our Lord Jesus Christ, who has blessed us with every spiritual blessing in the heavenly in Christ, just as He chose us in Him before the foundation of the world, that we should be holy and blameless before Him..."

The first question that should cross our minds for our study of these verses is: "What is the relationship of the people to God the Father?" He is mentioned first. Are we linked to God on nothing other than God's choice of us? Or does the passage hinge on believing God? If based on faith, and I think I have made a strong case that this is so, and the evidence will grow stronger as we move along, then all subsequent verses make sense yet leave man's free will choice to believe intact. The text does not lead to an esoteric group that God chose in Christ. Who is Paul talking about? He is talking about believers, those who believe God.

God the Father has blessed us (those who truly believe Him) with every spiritual blessing in Christ. He chose us in the Son so that we should be holy and blameless. God decided to do this (for those who believe Him) before He set the world in place. For without being in the Son, the One Who came in the flesh, we would never be Holy and blameless before God. (OT saints share in this because they too lived by faith in God.) (*Parenthesis, added.*)

The hour that God chose us in Christ poses no problem because the Scriptures teach that God knows all things at all times. He surely would have known at the pre-dawn of creation those who would believe Him, before they did so.

The key question to the whole first chapter is whether we need to believe God, the One Who sent Christ. If so all the rest of the chapter includes the benefits that accrue to the one who believes God. I think the church at Ephesus would read the text that way. More so since there were those in that city who had believed God for a span of their life before coming to Christ. Plus there is the fact that they only had the OT Scriptures; such makes this line of logic all that more likely to stand under the scrutiny of those who want to be true to the Word.

Further on Paul writes the following.

Eph 1:4b-6 -- "In love He predestined us to adoption as sons through Jesus Christ to Himself, according to the kind intention of His will, to the praise of the glory of His grace, which He freely bestowed on us in the beloved."

If this passage is rooted by faith in God as a starting point, then the word "predestined" can follow without the elect being some people God chose by His fiat alone. God chose all of us who believe Him before the dawn of the world, so we would have salvation. He planned for all those who believe Him to be adopted as sons through Jesus Christ to Himself.

The path that His people trod starts with believing God. And God provides them salvation through belief in His Son. But before any faith in Christ came to pass, God had decreed what would take place for those who believe Him. And of course God did this at the pleasure of His will.

We have no standing before Him that warrants that He act on our behalf. He is not required to give a single thing to those who simply believe Him. He is indebted to no man. We are all sinners, and still have a sin nature until we put our faith in Christ. God chose to declare us righteous by faith in Christ.

All theologians that teach strict "free will," at least those that I have read, hold the view that God had to foreknow our decision to believe in Christ. I don't think that quite squares with what is taking place in this context, nor throughout the NT. God chooses and God predestines; the act of being born again is by the will of God (Jn 1:12-13). God chose what those Who believed Him had to do; we must put our faith in Christ. But He knows those who believe and love Him, He knows us intimately; but we are not adopted as sons until we have faith in Christ. Only God knows those who truly believe Him and He will go to the ends of the earth to get the good news about Christ to that person.

This reasoning gains more support from further texts in Ephesians.

> Eph 1:18-20 – I pray that the eyes of your heart may be enlightened, so that you will know what is the hope of His calling, what are the riches of the glory of His inheritance in the saints, and <u>what is the surpassing greatness of His power toward us who believe.</u> These are in accordance with the working of the strength of His might which He brought about in Christ, when He raised Him from the dead and seated Him at His right hand in the heavenly places. . .

Paul writes in these three verses about those who *"believe,"* but the One doing the action in these verses is God. Does the verb *"believe"* here begin with God? Once again the action is continuous or repeated; it does not refer simply to faith in Christ. Salvation is an act of God for those who believe Him. They are predestined to have faith in Christ. God has chosen us in Christ.

This is how Paul would reason from the OT. However, it was much easier for him to do so in that day. He dealt with many people who formerly had faith in God, loved God, and then were drawn by the Father to have faith in Christ. Of course God supervised Paul, and worded the text, as He wanted it worded. I think his letter was much clearer to the people of that day. Should we not read the text in the same way today?

Let's go to another contested text in Ephesians.

> Eph 2:8-9 -- "For by grace you have been saved through faith; and that not of yourselves, it is the gift of God; not as a result of works, that no one may boast."

Some have used these two verses to assert the claim that God gives people the faith to be saved. They say the "it" here refers to faith.

Not so, according to Greek scholars (H. Alford, 1958). The grammar of the original text does not permit this interpretation. He states that the *"it"* is in the Greek neuter while both grace and faith are feminine. Hence *"it"* refers to the whole of salvation.

But with the proposed concept in this book the *"it"* can stand for all that goes before, including faith, as long as that faith is in Christ. Since belief starts with God, then God can give us all that it takes to be saved including faith in His Son, and this is indeed through His grace. For He has predestined those that believe Him to have faith in the One Who was sent and shed His blood for all mankind, if one would but believe.

I end the study of the letter to Ephesus here. The balance of the text over the first two chapters becomes self-explanatory once we apply the basic concept of "faith to faith."

Chapter Six

Paul's Doctrine of Salvation

in

Romans

Compared to his letter to the Church at Ephesus, Paul seemed to have a different purpose in mind when he wrote his treatise to those in Rome. He knew what the church in Ephesus had been taught. He was less aware of what the people in Rome had heard from any teacher of the Word who may have come their way.

So Paul, most likely, sought to explain the good news about Christ in full, to make redemption crystal clear so that there would be no mistake. The thrust of his letter to them describes what takes place in the lives of those who come to Christ. Toward this aim, Paul probes the depth and breadth of the doctrine of salvation. Even the scope of time and the plight of Man through history do not elude his attention.

Because Paul was so thorough we cannot go wrong if we let his letter to Rome be the crucible that helps us test the merits of this approach. Hence, the thesis here will rise or fall on the basis of what Paul writes in this epistle. If "faith to faith" is a central theme for those in Christ, then we should find this concept spelled out in Romans, more so than any other place in the Word. Will we find this to be the case?

Paul's Summary Statement to the Roman Epistle

I suggest that we once again walk in the footsteps of those that only had access to the Scriptures of the OT, and then read this letter from Paul? Might I also suggest that we take the place of those that believed, loved God for a time, and then heard about and came to Christ? Some parts of the book of Romans are much easier to grasp if we read with this mindset.

In fact Paul may speak to this very thing in the first chapter. He writes a précis of what is to come in his letter with a statement that had a profound impact on Martin Luther.

> Rom 1:16-17 -- "For I am not ashamed of the gospel, for it is the power of God for salvation to everyone who believes, to the Jew first and also to the Greek. For in it the righteousness of God is revealed from faith to faith; as it is written, 'But the righteous shall live by faith.'" (NASB)

The second verse led Martin Luther to realize that we are saved by the grace of God through faith. None the less, this servant of the Lord, to whom we are all so indebted, never fully dealt with the "faith to faith" part of this passage, at least to my knowledge. Hence, he came very close to what was later taught by Calvin advocates. Luther even had a long and sharp dispute with Erasmus, about whether Man has any voice in being saved. And his "The Bondage of the Will" (1525, trans. 1990) says that since we have a depraved and sinful nature we cannot come to Christ. God must give us His grace so that we can have faith in Christ and be saved. God chooses us.

But might the phrase "*faith to faith*" teach us something a little different? And to add to this premise, the verb form that Paul uses for "*believe*" in this précis states nearly the same thing. The action in the Greek is continual or repeated. In the same context as the phrase "*faith to faith*" the verb should most likely be seen as repeated action.

Be aware, too, that the quote, "*But the righteous shall live by faith*" is from Habakkuk 2:4. And when we put this statement into the context of the OT prophet, the faith proclaimed there did not read as a single action or one point in time. Hence we have a third clue from Paul that repeated or continual faith is a key concept for his letter.

Since Paul alerts us three times to repeated or continual faith in his summary of what is to come in his letter, we best take great care when we read what follows. In fact, the theme "*faith to faith*" may be an essential phrase to help us discern what Paul intends and what God has said to us. This is the light that will guide us as we study the most puzzling parts of his treatise to Rome.

So what might the phrase "*faith to faith*" mean? The New International Version (NIV) does not say "*faith to faith.*" Rather this more recent version of the Bible translates the Greek as "*faith, first to last.*" From what I understand the original language is best rendered as "*faith to faith.*"

Scholars can miss truth when they do not agree on, or know, what an original text means. The risk of harm is much greater if by chance they are the ones who translate the Greek and Hebrew into a new language, or a new version. We all have a penchant to want to make words say what makes sense to us. Translations close to the Greek text are more apt to capture what the author intends.

To change the wording, as done in the NIV, seems to weaken the meaning of the text. The slight shift in emphasis may cost us a true understanding of what Paul writes. And as we have seen before, the phrase may have profound consequence for what is taught elsewhere, not just in Romans.

But I must admit and point out that good commentaries do not agree on the meaning of *"faith to faith."* Bible scholars are all over the place. Some say the phrase is ambiguous. Some say it refers to Old and New Testament faith. Some say it is going from faith for salvation to living by faith. Some say the text refers to the Gospel being given from person to person. Others say the phrase means something else, most all of them suspect and vague in detail.

No commentary explains the phrase in the way that I will suggest here, at least none that I have read. There is one author, C. Olson (2002) in his book, "Beyond Calvinism and Arminianism," who implies that this phrase may be at root for how we come to faith in Christ. He thinks of the first step as "repentance faith," but he failed to demonstrate in his book how this thought fits with any of the key texts in Romans. He explains all texts in Romans as most freewill scholars do. There may be a much better way to go.

If *"faith to faith"* is vital to Paul's teaching, then the phrase needs to be reasoned out in the light of what Paul writes later on in his letter. The "repentance faith" of Olson dilutes what Paul intends. Yet his comments give credence to the idea that the phrase may have more significance for the Good News than most think; and if so then these three words should help those in Rome gain insight into what Paul writes to them. Such a phrase in a summary of what is to come should be seen as key to the inspired thinking that God gave to Paul.

As Paul moves through his letter to Rome he makes a transition from OT faith in God to NT faith in Christ. The phrase *"faith to faith"* may be key to grasping his logic in the progression. And since Paul is talking about the Gospel then there could be more significance than just this transition. When we get to chapters eight and nine of Romans the phrase may be critical as we wrestle with what Paul writes. These texts are less formidable and less confusing if read with the mindset of *"faith to faith."*

Paul often draws a distinction between God and Christ. Though Paul is clear that Christ is One with God. Let's look at his salutation to see the roles in the Godhead. Note his words:

Rom 1:1-7 -- "Paul, a bond-servant of Christ Jesus, called as an apostle, set apart for the gospel of God which He promised before through His prophets, in the Holy Scriptures concerning His Son... to all who are beloved of God in Rome, called as saints: Grace to you and peace from God our Father and the Lord Jesus Christ."

Look next at two more verses early in the letter to the people of Rome that lend more support for the "faith to faith" concept.

Rom 3:21-22 -- "But now apart from the Law the righteousness of God has been manifested, being witnessed by the Law and the Prophets, even the righteousness of God through faith in Jesus Christ for all those who believe; for there is no distinction..."

These two verses are far short of conclusive but the text deserves a close look. Is the *"faith"* here the same as what Paul means by *"believe?"* If they refer precisely to the same thing then the reading is quite awkward. But at times wording in a new language can seem less than clear. Hence to translate correctly one must have some idea about what is being said.

If we should read this verse as *"faith to faith"* then the text is much easier to grasp. To support this idea the Greek word for *"believe,"* as we have seen elsewhere, once again speaks to repeated or continuous action. Such lends more leverage to our assessment. We should not make much of this unless we find more evidence of the same throughout the book of Romans. So follow with me.

The God Who Justifies

A few verses later Paul goes to the OT Scriptures to show how God deemed people as righteous in those days.

> Rom 4:3-5 -- "For what does the Scripture say? 'Abraham believed God, and it was credited to him as righteousness.' Now to the one who works, his wage is not credited as a favor, but as what is due. But to the one who does not work, but believes in Him who justifies the ungodly, his faith is credited as righteousness..."

Here we find the belief of Abraham, but he believes God, *"Him who justifies."* Keep the *"belief"* mentioned here in mind for later. Put a huge bookmark or red flag at this place in Romans, and at this page in this book. Later we will find the phrase *"God is the one who justifies,"* linked directly to the elect (cf. Rm 8:33).

Paul also gives us the exact point in time when God will justify us.

> Rom 3:23-26 -- "For all have sinned and fall short of the glory of God, being justified as a gift by His grace

through the redemption which is in Christ Jesus; whom God displayed publicly as a propitiation in His blood through faith. This was to demonstrate His righteousness, because in the forbearance of God He passed over the sins previously committed; for the demonstration, I say, of His righteousness at the present time, so that He would be just and the justifier of the one who has faith in Jesus."

Study Paul's thoughts about OT faith (Rom 4) before going on. The passage speaks of faith in God and in Christ. Then towards the end of chapter four Paul starts a passage that may be the **most critical for our entire study in this book.** Here we begin to see Paul's reasoning of "faith to faith."

Rom 4:23-5:2 -- "Now not for his (Abraham's) sake only was it written, that it was credited to him, but for our sake also, to whom it will be credited, as those who believe in Him who raised Jesus our Lord from the dead, He who was delivered up because of our transgressions, and was raised because of our justification. Therefore having been justified by faith, we have peace with God through our Lord Jesus Christ, through whom also we have obtained our introduction by faith into this grace in which we stand and we exult in hope of the glory of God."

I have underlined the key points. Note that Paul talks about his own belief ("our") in the One "who raised Jesus our Lord from the dead." This "One" is none other than God the Father, not just Christ. Later in the passage Paul talks of more faith, but this faith introduces us into grace. When we compare this last "faith" to the "faith" of Romans 3:21-22 and 3:26, quoted above, we find that this faith is in Jesus Christ. Without the "faith to faith" concept we would miss what Paul was saying.

The question now begins to spur more interest and excitement. How is faith in God, the One Who justifies, linked to faith in Christ, especially since God justifies us when we put our faith in Christ? How and why should we go from one to the other? Are they the same or are they different? We will deal with this in Romans, chapters eight and nine.

The Spirit of God and the Spirit of Christ

Before we go to the most challenging texts in Romans, look at a passage that comes first in chapter eight. Paul does a careful blending of the *"Spirit of God"* and the *"Spirit of Christ"* (cf Rom 8:9-11). Paul minces no words with those at Rome.

He told his readers that if they thought that they had the Spirit of God yet did not have the Spirit of Christ then they did not belong to God. Might this mean that true faith in God is certain to lead to true faith in Christ? And again, before the Gospel message the people of that day would not have fully grasped this idea. Faith in Christ was hidden and a mystery until that time.

Now the question becomes, how does God make certain that we have the Spirit of Christ? And in a special way the issue is crucial for those who believe God in Rome. Paul's readers were faced with whether to put their faith in Christ. Can God lose some along the way in the transition (cf Jn 6:39-40). Are these people just naturally going to believe in Christ? How does Paul deal with this perplexing question?

How might this impact us today? Will those who truly believe God not come to faith in Christ, the One who was sent and died on our behalf to pay the penalty for our sin? Can God, the One Who sent His Son, have one flock of sheep that believe Him and Christ have another flock that believe Him? We must remember that they are One.

The Difficult Texts of Romans

Let's go now to the texts at root of the never-ending debate that extends back to the days of Augustine. Read with the "sandal test" in mind, as a person who first believed God and then later came to faith in Christ. And whom would Paul be writing to in Rome other than people with this kind of background and OT mindset?

We will look first at Romans 8:28-33. The best way to follow with me is to go to your Bible and read the entire passage beginning in 8:28. Do this in the NASB as this version is used here and is close to the Greek language. After you have read the entire passage a few times then return here and we will go through the text a verse at a time.

> Rom 8:28 -- "And we know that God causes all things to work together for good to those who love God, to those who are called according to His purpose."

Note that Christ is not mentioned in this verse. Paul writes about the relationship with God as *"to those who love God."* The phrase *"to those who love God"* is juxtaposed with the phrase *" to those who are called according to His purpose."* Paul then explains in the next two verses how this *"called according to His purpose"* is going to take shape in the lives of those who love God. God's purpose is spelled out in verses 29 and 30.

> Rom 8:29 -- "For those whom He foreknew, He also predestined to become conformed to the image of His Son, so that He would be the firstborn among many brethren."

I think the word *"foreknew"* here means exactly that. God foreknew them by their true faith in Him, not by their faith in Christ. Then Paul mentions the Son of God.

We can stumble, fret, and split hairs, over this verse many times. All free will scholars say that God had to foreknow our faith in Christ. The text does not read this way. To compare text with text study what John says in his Epistle which we looked at before (1 Jn 5:1-10). John taught that if we truly believe God we will put our faith in Christ.

One might contend that this is not the right interpretation since Paul writes about love; and that surely cannot be a condition. I agree with this, but Paul is talking about the results of true faith at each step. No faith is mentioned in any of these verses.

Study has convinced me that the word *"foreknew"* means more than simple "knowledge of." The text implies an intimate knowing. Most scholars agree with this. Calvin scholars see this as one of the prime reasons that the elect are chosen by God before they come to faith in Christ. This seems to be the case; but if we are dealing with a "faith to faith" concept, then the word *"foreknew"* is a perfect fit.

Truly believing God logically precedes faith in Christ, His Son. How are we to believe the Lamb of God if we do not believe the One Who sent Him? How can we know we need a Savior if we don't know God? He predestines those He foreknew to be conformed to the image of the Son, Who is God with us in bodily form, Immanuel; the One Who redeemed us by His death. The same people that believe the One Who sent the Son will believe in the Son. God has ordained this to be so.

When we read the passage with the mindset of someone that once believed God and then accepts Christ, the passage becomes quite clear. And those in Rome, to whom Paul wrote, fit within this mindset. And, if we only had OT Scriptures, and none of the NT, we would derive this way of reading the text too. For us today with the entire NT in our hands, the text is much harder to grasp.

Rom 8:30 -- "And these whom He predestined, He
also called; and these whom He called, He also
justified; and these whom He justified, He also
glorified."

God calls those whom He knows, those that believe Him,
with His Gospel. True belief implies love for God. (This is the
same as God's call in 2 Thes 2:14.) I think, as many do, that the
"*call*" in verse 30 cannot be resisted, but this call is certain to
get an answer from the person because they believe God. God
will lose no one who believes. All who truly believe God the
Father will come to faith in Christ. God adopts those that
believe Him by giving them new life in Christ.

Those who love (believe and want a relationship with) God
will put their faith in Christ. Faith in Him is our justification
because of what He did for us, and in the end we will be
glorified. We are indeed secure. Security begins with God. Out
of His grace God promises that those who truly believe Him will
receive the gift of salvation that comes through faith in Christ.

Rom 8:31-32 -- "What then shall we say to these
things? If God is for us, who is against us? He who
did not spare His own Son, but delivered Him up for us
all, how will He not also with Him freely give us all
things?"

God freely gives those who belong to Him all things and this
includes His Son. Salvation is indeed a gift from God. He
predestines those who believe and know Him to be in His Son.
But we will not be on the receiving end unless we believe and
commit to God, the One Who sent the Son.

Rom 8:33 -- "Who will bring a charge against **God's
elect**? God is the one who justifies."

Where before in Romans have we seen the words, "*God is
the one who justifies*"? I asked you to put a bookmark or red

flag at a place a few pages back. Where has the "belief" gone that is mentioned in two places in Romans chapter four? Let me repeat the verses:

> Rom 4:3-5 -- "For what does the Scripture say? And Abraham believed God, and it was credited to him as righteousness. Now to the one who works, his wage is not credited as a favor, but as what is due. But to the one who does not work, but believes in Him who justifies the ungodly, his faith is credited as righteousness.

> Rom 4:24 -- "...but for our sake also, to whom it will be credited, as those who believe in Him who raised Jesus our Lord from the dead."

The "Him" in these verses refers to God the Father. But God does not justify us, that is give us salvation, without faith in His Son. But does God require us to make two decisions of faith? Does He not turn all that have faith in Him over to the Son? As Christ said "...thine they were and thou gavest them to me..." (Jn 17:6).

When we study these verses in Romans chapter four and the progression of Paul's thought over the next pages it seems fairly clear to me that God's elect are those who truly believe God. One of the questions that Paul deals with in his discourse is how do we go from faith in God to faith in Christ. And more, how does God not lose any of those who belong to Him in the process.

God has ordained that all who truly believe Him will have salvation. This is basic to what is said in the OT and also what Paul writes in the fourth chapter and the first part of the fifth chapter in Romans. But we must have faith in Christ. God cannot depend on us to make that happen because we may be so dense that we do not even know we need to do this. But if we truly believe God He will reveal the Son to us; but many like Paul kick against the goads (Acts 26:14).

Perhaps this is the reason why Paul says that those who truly believe God are the "*elect*." God makes certain that they take that next step of faith for salvation. God chose them to take that step before the earth was formed. All who truly believe God will end up with faith in Christ. God will lose no one who belongs to Him by faith. He has turned all things over to the Son. The Holy Spirit will be powerful when we truly believe God, both to convict us of sin and to convince us that the answer to our sin problem before God is Christ, the Lamb of God.

Would this not be exceedingly good news to those believers in Rome who knew God before but did not yet know Christ? And if He can choose us in the Son will He not make certain that all other blessings promised in Christ will come to pass too. What a miraculous work of God, for we have experienced the proof of His plan in our lives! And He has sealed us in Christ with the Holy Spirit of promise (Eph 1:13). We have been adopted by His will.

Paul goes on in the eighth chapter to explain our security in Christ (Rom 8:33-39). When God plants us in Christ, He already knows for certain that we believe Him. We belong to Him by faith and we have passed from death to life. He gives us to His Son. And when God plants someone in His Son the rest of His work in us is also certain to come to completion. In the end we will be glorified. Nothing can separate us from His love.

Rom 8:33-35a & 8:38-39 -- "Who will bring a charge against God's elect? God is the one who justifies; who is the one who condemns? Christ Jesus is He who died, yes, rather who was raised, who is at the right hand of God, who also intercedes for us. Who will separate us from the love of Christ? ... For I am convinced that neither death, nor life, nor angels, nor principalities, nor things present, nor things to come, nor powers, nor height, nor depth, nor any other created thing, will be able to separate us from the love of God, which is in Christ Jesus our Lord."

To sum up the difficult passage in the eighth chapter, all those with true faith in God are His elect. We must choose to believe. If we truly believe God He calls us to put our faith in Christ for salvation and we will do so. Those who believe God will heed His call to come to Christ.

Hence God calls them the elect and they continue to be His elect for all of life and beyond. Those who say that they have faith in God yet do not accept Christ and His work on the cross do not truly believe God. For as Paul says if we think we have the Spirit of God yet do not have the Spirit of Christ we do not belong to God (Rom 8:9).

We can never guess who the elect may be, or who they will be. God is the only One who knows who truly believes Him, for He knows the heart. Might this be the reason that Paul talks about God searching the heart immediately before he goes through the steps in God's plan for those He foreknew (cf Rom 8:27)? But once there is true faith we are indeed secure, He will give us our position in the Son. He adopts us; we are born again by His will and by His Spirit. We will never lose our position in Christ.

For most people today faith in God and in God the Son take place almost simultaneously. But that may not have been the case for many of those whom Paul was trying to reach. But God knew them and did not abandon them. We can never be sure that anyone believes God until they put their faith in Christ. But we know that if they choose not to do so they call God a liar (1 Jn 5:1-10).

Salvation and the Jewish Remnant

What can we say about Romans 9:6ff? This passage is much tougher to digest. Many debate the nuances of meaning. Let's see what happens when we use the "sandal test." I would add but one comment before we look at the text. The Romans 9 passage seems to be a repeat of Romans 8:28ff, now in different words and applied only to the Jews. Beginning at verse 9:6:

> Rom 9:6-9 -- "But it is not as though the word of God has failed. For they are not all Israel who are descended from Israel; nor are they all children because they are Abraham's descendants, but: 'Through Isaac your descendants will be named.' That is, it is not the children of the flesh who are children of God, but the children of the promise are regarded as descendants. For this is a word of promise: 'At this time I will come, and Sarah shall have a son.'"

Some scholars of a "free will" bent say that this text refers to the nation of Israel, not to individuals. There is some evidence that this may be so. But for the subject at hand, when read with the proposed mindset, I doubt that it makes any difference.

The *"children of promise"* are a subset of the group called *"those who love God,"* spoken of in 8:28. The people of this subset are those true believers that were from among the Jews. Note once again that Christ is not yet seen in the text. These people believe God and His promise.

Then a hotly debated passage comes next.

> Rom 9:10-13 -- "And not only this, but there was Rebekah also, when she had conceived twins by one man, our father Isaac; for though the twins were not yet born, and had not done anything good or bad, so that God's purpose according to His choice would stand, not because of works, but because of Him who calls, it

was said to her, 'The older will serve the younger;' Just
as it is written 'Jacob I loved, but Esau I hated.'"

These few verses are an OT instance of what Paul meant by
"those called according to His purpose" (cf Rom 8:28). The
purpose mentioned is for the older to <u>serve</u> the younger. Paul
says nothing about faith or promise in this case. Rather he
speaks of God calling for the purpose of service.

When we combine the last two quotes we have a replica of
Romans 8:28. *"those who love God"*(children of the promise
and of faith) are side by side with *"those called according to His
purpose."*

The next verses in Chapter Nine tell us that God will grant
mercy to whom He desires to grant mercy. And we know that
His mercy and grace come through the One promised. And we
also know from prior claims in Romans that God grants mercy to
those who truly believe Him. Those who do not believe will not
receive mercy. In fact they will harden and reject Christ. Paul
includes what happens to those who do not believe God, because
he is teaching about what will happen to the Jewish people who
do not live by faith.

Now continue with Paul's thoughts.

Rom 9:14-18 -- "What shall we say then? There is no
injustice with God, is there? May it never be! For He
says to Moses, 'I will have mercy on whom I have
mercy and I will have compassion on whom I have
compassion.' So then it does not depend on the man
who wills or the man who runs, but on God who has
mercy. For the Scriptures says to Pharaoh, 'For this
very purpose I raised you up, to demonstrate My power
in you, and that My name might be proclaimed
throughout the whole earth.' So then He has mercy on
whom He desires and he hardens whom He desires."

So God will work out His purpose in the *"children of promise,"* (those who believe Him). He will grant mercy to them just as He did to those who truly believe God in verse 8:28. He will do all the same things for them that Paul writes about in 8:29-30. Out of God's mercy the Son paid the penalty for their sin. They will be deemed to be righteous before Him as they put their faith in the Son. They will be conformed to the image of the Son and they will be glorified. But those who do not believe God, He will harden.

Paul then comments about God as the potter. These are tough verses to get our minds around. The potter passage refers back to OT Scripture. In Jeremiah (Jer 18) the potter, Who was God, shaped vessels according to the make up of the clay. There, the clay referred to nations.

In Isaiah (Is 29:15-16) the clay refers to people. This OT prophet taught that the clay is not equal to the potter. He says that what is made should not say to its maker – *"He did not make me"* or *"He has no understanding."* And in Isaiah 45 the thought is *"Woe to the one who quarrels with His maker,"* and asks, *"What are you doing?"*

The potter is free to work with the clay as he sees fit. God as potter can deal with people however He wants. The clay is His. But earlier in Romans Paul tells us how God will deal with the clay, on the basis of His promise of salvation to those that believe Him. The latter is implied in the passage but not stated. The clay has no footing to quarrel with God for what He does or how He does it. God has established the way in which He works, and He shapes all things after His will.

God as potter is also going to work out His purpose through two distinct kinds of vessels (Rom 9:22-24). There are those that believe Him and those that do not. He endures the one and He bestows grace and mercy on the other. The potter is going to work with both believing Jews and Gentiles in the same way.

Rom 9:22-24 -- "What if God, although willing to demonstrate His wrath and to make His power known, endured with much patience vessels of wrath prepared for destruction? And He did so to make known the riches of His glory upon vessels of mercy, which He prepared beforehand for glory, even us, whom He also called, not from among Jews only, but also from among Gentiles."

The last verses of the ninth chapter of Romans seem to summarize what has gone before in the passages quoted above.

Rom 9:30-32 -- "What shall we say then? That Gentiles, who did not pursue righteousness, attained righteousness, even the righteousness which is by faith; but Israel, pursuing a law of righteousness, did not arrive at that law. Why? Because they did not pursue it by faith, but as though it were by works. They stumbled over the stumbling stone...."

Further on, in Chapter 11, Paul addressed the lack of faith by the Jews. He tells us, "...they were broken off for their unbelief, but you stand by your faith" (Rom 11:20). And then Paul adds that God would respond to them again if they turned to belief (Rom 11:23). They needed to believe God and accept His Son.

God's Purpose for the Elect (Comparing OT and NT)

I must say a few more things about Romans 8:28 and 9:10-13. The "called according to His purpose" is a critical part of what God does in these verses. What is God's purpose for those who believe Him?

Paul spells out this purpose in verses 8:29 and 8:30. God predestined those He foreknew to be conformed to the image of His Son. He justified them. And He will glorify them. These things are certain to happen, just as certain as what God's choosing for the purpose of service meant in the OT.

But of great importance for all the Scriptures, and expressly for shedding light on the texts of Romans 8 and 9, God could not choose people in the OT on the basis of faith in Christ. This faith was still a mystery and hidden, yet future. So could there have been a basis for how God could choose people in the OT for His purpose. Might He have known that they believed Him, God the Father?

And the Hebrew word used in the OT about God knowing them before they were born is "yada," most commonly an intimate knowing. And yes, if God chose them based on what He knew about them, He would have known of their belief in Him before their birth. Hence, He can choose them for any purpose that He desires, but only one kind of vessel, those that believe Him, are destined for their good. God grants them salvation and transforms their belief in Him to faith in the Son. He turns all things over to the Son.

The NT Jewish author, Paul, uses the same OT principle to show how God gives the gift of salvation, "faith in Christ," during the days of Christ on earth and then after the cross. This is why the elect of God, are those who truly believe God, and they will put their faith in Christ. They are certain to do so, and if they never do they never believed God in the first place. As has been said before, they make Him a liar (cf 1 Jn 5:1-10).

Then we have more of what God plans in Romans 9:23. God wants *"to make known the riches of His glory upon vessels of mercy which He prepared for glory."*

We are His and He will cause all to work together for good to those who are His. We indeed have access to the riches of His glory that He wants to lavish on us. We are a people for God's own possession. And He delights in doing things for His people. And nothing comes our way that does not do so by His

permission. He literally gives us salvation when we believe
Him. And if we let Him, He will teach us from His Word and
help us to mature and grow. His Word will transform us into the
people that He desires us to be, conformed to the image of His
Son. We are alive to God in Christ Jesus (Rom 6:11).

What about all the People who seem to believe and love God?

What can we say about those millions upon millions of
people who seem to believe God? And if you did not ask you
should have, for Paul answers this question. Some outwardly
appear to love Him. Why do they not end up in Christ? Is their
belief in and love for God not genuine? Paul speaks to this, at
least for the Hebrew people. For he says:

> Rom 10:1-4 -- "Brethren my heart's desire and my
> prayer to God for them is for their salvation. For I
> testify about them that they have zeal for God, but not
> in accordance with knowledge. For not knowing about
> God's righteousness and seeking to establish their own,
> they did not subject themselves to the righteousness of
> God. For Christ is the end of the law for righteousness
> to everyone who believes."

Paul said that the people who reject Christ, yet seem to have
a love for God, really do not love Him. They have zeal for
something that they think is God, but in reality their god is not
God. He is not the God of the Scriptures. These people have
neither a high enough view of God nor a low enough view of
Man.

They create a god in the imagination of their mind rather
than accept Who God really is. They might have zeal and appear
to love. But if they fail to believe what God says about Himself
in His Word, then their faith is vain, for they have faith in a god

of their own wishful thinking. Faith is only as good as the object of that faith.

The fatal error in what they know of God is that they have the wrong view of His righteousness. He can tolerate no sin in His presence. He is infinitely pure and Holy. The only righteousness that He can allow into His presence is that which is perfect. The only one to meet that standard is His Son; the One He sent; the One Who is fully God and fully man.

Our own works will never measure up. We will always fall short. Hence, God provides His Son. God offers this Lamb without blemish to us. He gives us His Son's life, unstained by sin, so that we can be adopted, to be sons of God. Our faith in Christ becomes our righteousness so that the Holy Spirit can live within us. And after death we can go to be with God.

Most people who have a zeal for god fail to understand how God sees our sin. They think that somehow their own righteous deeds will pave the way to God and heaven. They do not believe that salvation comes from God, not from us. Or they may try to substitute the rituals of a church for what God wants to give us. They say that God will honor and accept their works; so they substitute human effort or church rites for what God has done for us. Hence they reject God's only Son, the One Who knew no sin. They spurn the thought that Christ paid with His life on the cross, the cruelest of deaths that human kind could perpetrate. And they do not believe God's witness to His Son.

What is so often the case they do not believe that God will bestow His mercy and grace on them; rather they try to earn God's favor with works of their own hands. Such is futile. Any taint of sin requires total justice; we deserve to be banished forever from God's presence. Yet God loved us while we were yet sinners and set the cross before us. He wants to give us the righteousness of God through His Son. But we must believe God, and if we truly believe God we will accept His Son, for God has said to do so.

Do we bow at the Savior's feet, or do we shake our heads and pass by in disbelief? God justifies us when we put our faith in Christ, declaring us forever not guilty, fully innocent, before Him, no matter the depth, breadth, or massive weight of our sin. And by raising Christ from the dead, God has said that the cross is enough. At the cross our old sin nature has been put to death and we have eternal life in Him.

The last quoted verse from Romans shouts all the more for the need to present the God of the Word to all that do not know Him. If we convey a defective picture of Who God is we add to the risk that people will resist Him. And if they do not believe Him and grasp that we are total sinners before Him then they will never accept Jesus. We must proclaim that God loves all people and wants all to be saved. If God gives no genuine choice to sinners who hear the message, He surely does not love the whole world. But Jesus felt sorrow over the Holy City since the people would not come to Him (Mt 23:37).

And Paul said that the word of faith that he preaches is:

Rom 10:9-10 -- "that if you confess with your mouth Jesus as Lord, and believe in your heart that God raised Him from the dead, you will be saved; for with the heart man believes, resulting in righteousness, and with the mouth he confesses resulting in salvation."

Summary of Romans

As a way of summing up the book of Romans let me quote what Christ declared in the Gospel of John.

Jn 17:3 -- *"This is eternal life, that they may know You, the only true God, and Jesus Christ whom You have sent."*

Although John never uses the phrase "faith to faith" as Paul does, his theology is much the same as Paul's. John said that if we love the Father we will love the Son of God too (cf. 1 Jn 5:1-12). God's message to all people is that eternal life results from faith in His Son. Do we believe what God says? If we do we will put our faith in Christ as the answer to our sin problem before Him.

Scholars have neglected to deal with the faith in God to the faith in Christ issue. And this is so despite the essential truths that Paul spells out in his summary remarks leading into the book of Romans (Rom 1:16-17).

We have salvation by faith in the Son, for that is what Christ came to give us. When we believe God He predestines us to have faith in Christ so that we might be adopted as His sons, and conformed to the image of Christ, to live with Him forever. We become part of His family. Once adopted we are His from that time forward. Like being born into this world, we cannot be unborn. God has set His purpose on us who believe Him. He gives Christ to us and He gives us to Christ. And He intends to sum up all things in Christ, things in heaven and things upon the earth (Eph 1:9-10). He has put all things under the Lordship of Christ, and Christ belongs to God (1 Cor 3:21-23).

This ends my review and thought on what Paul teaches about the term "elect." Some of the key Scriptures are hard to understand. But "faith to faith" seems to be the best way to read the texts in question. When I go to these Scriptures with this concept in mind many hard to grasp passages make much more sense to me.

The elect are those who truly believe God, and such faith is verified when we put our faith in Christ for salvation. Those who are saved believe God through faith in Christ (1 Pt 1:21).

Chapter Seven

Faith and Purpose in the
Old Testament

"Does God the Father cause us to believe Him or only to have faith in the Son of God?" Scholars of theology have not dealt with this question as far as I have been able to discern from what has been written. But this is vital to the whole debate on free will.

Those who have written on this issue have only focused on faith in Christ, those that are saved. But over half the Bible, and the only Scriptures they had at the time the NT was written, pointed to Abraham; and he believed God.

Might salvation, faith in Christ, be predestined by God, while believing God is not caused by Him. Scholars have ignored this part of the equation. They just might have the wrong view of the elect. But Calvin doctrine demands that we rule this out. They have not done so.

Nor can they do so. Nor did Augustine address this issue to my knowledge but that is a fatal mistake to the way they read the Scriptures. The Word, both Old and New Testaments, is silent on this key matter.

Calvin scholars take their derived point of view back into the OT where we see the sovereign rule of God as He shapes the march of history to conform to His set path. Since God reigns over all these events and all those involved, they reason that God also rules in who believes and trusts Him, not just the Son. Does this premise hold up when we search through the varied texts of the OT?

To come close to an answer to this question we need to survey those Scriptures that speak to this premise. We will look at what God knows and when He knows it. Second, we will look at faith and trust as described by God's spokesmen in the age before Christ. Third we will look at why God chose certain people in the OT. Then we will do some prudent analysis of how God seems to fashion His plan while we are still free to choose to believe. Last we will tackle some puzzling OT texts that some of God's servants quote in the books of the NT.

As a whole the OT presents many awesome accounts of God knowing and God choosing. And the precise hour that God does both astounds all that hear the Word. Yet He chose all the featured people for a set purpose, some for serving God as those who belong to Him; and He chose a few to bring Him glory in other ways. I have found none that go beyond the scope of these limits. Nowhere in the books of the OT can we find a statement, passage or verse that says God causes us to believe Him.

Hence, we cannot presume that God gave faith to a select few. He could just as well choose someone for a service before their birth, since He would have known if and when that person would come to true faith in Him. We must be careful not to confuse knowing and causing. Knowing is on the side of omniscience, while choosing is on the side of God's causing. We must always stay alert to see if and when the texts draw a distinction between the two.

Paul said (Rom 9:22-23) that God knows and works with two kinds of vessels. He prepares some for glory and some for destruction. The first are those people that believe Him and the second are those that do not. And Paul implies too that God will work as a potter on these two kinds of vessels to shape His will on earth for His glory and for the good of those who are His. Hence, we should be able to go to the canon of the OT and find that such is the case.

God Knows Us Intimately

Before we look at what the writers of that day said about God's choosing some to serve let's first review how well God knows us. His servants of old claim that God has detailed knowledge of all our life, long before we are born. This is rock bottom basic, a given that no one who knows Scripture would dare to try and refute. The passages that support this solid truth are many and they include:

Ps 139:1-4 and 13-16 -- "O Lord, You have searched me and known me. You know when I sit down and when I rise up; You understand my thought from afar. You scrutinize my path and my lying down, and are intimately acquainted with all my ways. Even before there is a word on my tongue, behold, O Lord, You know it all." ... "For You formed my inward parts; You wove me in my mother's womb. I will give thanks to You, for I am fearfully and wonderfully made; wonderful are Your works, and my soul knows it very well. My frame was not hidden from You,

when I was made in secret, and skillfully wrought in
the depths of the earth. Your eyes have seen my
unformed substance; and in Your book were all written
the days that were ordained for me, when as yet there
was not one of them."

Jer 1:5 -- "Before I formed you in the womb I knew
you, and before you were born I consecrated you; I
have appointed you a prophet to the nations."

Such exhaustive and perfect knowledge transcends far
beyond what we can begin to conceive with our frail minds; God
knows each of us in a wonderful and intimate manner. He
knows all of our ways and all of our words; yes, before we even
open our mouths to speak. Nothing escapes His notice. Many
Scriptures substantiate this certainty. All students of the Word
who are honest with the texts accept these truths and honor and
praise God for Who He is.

We still must accept that to know is not the same thing as to
cause. In the Psalm quote above there is a blend of action verbs
ranging from those that refer to "knowing," to a few that point to
"causing." To know implies full perception, but with no fixed
control. To cause implies a sense of direct involvement and rule.

Those verbs above that go beyond knowing, attest that God
takes charge of what He has ordained to happen. In this, God
clearly says He has written our days. He has set the limits of our
life, for He rules over life and death, yet death would not have
come except for the fall of man. We all live on borrowed time,
by the mercy of God.

Read the Jeremiah quote; there are two aspects to what the
prophet writes. God both knew and He consecrated. Here we
seem to have God's action of control (consecrating) predicated
by what He knew. Some might think that this prophet used a
type of parallel thought that is common to Hebrew poetry; this of
course would blend the two aspects and make them have one

central idea. But when verbs have two distinct aims then they don't impart quite the same meaning. The question is, "What did God know?" Did He know that Jeremiah believed Christ? Paul said that faith in Christ was veiled in the OT.

Faith and Trust in the OT

Let's look now at a few texts in the OT that speak about faith and trust. There aren't many, but those that we find are heavily loaded with significance for NT thought.

The most quoted text in the NT on the theme of belief concerns Abraham. God came to Abraham in a vision and promised this OT saint that He would give him an heir. The Lord then took Abraham outside and showed him the heavens and the stars, and said, *"So shall your descendents be."*

> Gn 15:6 --   "Then he believed in the Lord; and He reckoned it to him as righteousness."

God deemed that the faith of this OT patriarch would be as righteousness. And God avowed this long before He gave the Law to Moses, 430 years on down the road. Three chapters after this first declaration, God said anew that all nations would be blessed in this OT saint (Gn 18:18).

We dare not ignore the fact on this issue that there is no place in the archives of the OT or NT where the Word says that God caused Abraham to believe Him, or that God gave Him faith. We can only build this case from an eisegesis reading; the Word is silent. Rather, Abraham believed God Who gave Him the promise. But He would not have claimed the promise of the One to come, if He did not first believe God. And likewise, if Abraham had failed to claim God's promise, this would have showed that he really did not believe God.

The second most quoted OT text on faith was written by Habakkuk, a man who lived in the last days of Judah just before the exile to Babylon. The occasion faced by this prophet prods him to ask a troubling question that plagues all thinking people. Where is the justice of God when wickedness abounds? And when this man of God heard that the Lord was going to punish Judah by the hand of the wicked Chaldeans, this aroused great alarm in his mind. How could God do this? Then God replied with some profound earth-shaking words that Paul used in the NT.

> Hab 2:4 -- "Behold, as for the proud one, his soul is not right within him; but the righteous will live by his faith."

The answer from the Lord stopped the prophet dead in his tracks. He could say and ask nothing more. Who are we to question God?

> Hab 2:20 -- "But the Lord is in His holy temple. Let all the earth be silent before Him."

This indeed is faith. There is none like God, and no one sits where He sits. Let God do what He does and be silent before Him. The prophet could do nothing but yield, humble himself and fully accept what the Lord was doing. He learned his lesson well, for pride and faith cannot co-exist in the same heart, without an odious mix, and that God will deal with.

Authors of the OT more commonly used the word "trust" than the word faith or believe. So let's look at a few passages that speak about trust.

> Job 13:15-16 -- "Though He slay me, I will hope (trust) in Him. Nevertheless I will argue my ways before Him. This also will be my salvation, for a godless man may not come before His presence."

Ps 56:11-14 -- "In God I have put my trust, I shall not be afraid. What can man do to me? Your vows are binding upon me, O God; I will render thank offerings to You. For You have delivered my soul from death, indeed my feet from stumbling, so that I may walk before God in the light of the living."

Prv 3:5-6 -- "Trust in the Lord with all your heart and do not lean on your own understanding. In all your ways acknowledge Him, and He will make your paths straight."

Jer 17:7-8 -- "Blessed is the man who trusts in the Lord and whose trust is the Lord. For he will be like a tree planted by the water, that extends its roots by a stream and will not fear when the heat comes; but its leaves will be green, and it will not be anxious in a year of drought nor cease to yield fruit."

Not one of these verses even hints that God gives people faith or trust in Him. Rather David says the trust was his own, saying *"my trust."* Of course the faith and trust of these verses includes more than just salvation. They speak for how we are to live out our relationship with God, in the light of Who He is and who we are not.

Choosing His Own People in the OT for Service

Plenty of confusion can muddle our thoughts when we read about God's sovereign choices in the OT; for God chose both those of faith and those without. And for each choice God had a purpose in mind. God worked with people who believed and loved Him, and He chose to use some who did not believe or love Him.

The way, and the end to which, God works His will in these two kinds of mortal vessels of this life are quite distinct (cf Rom 9:22-23). We must stay vigilant so that we do not void the wide gulf fixed between the two. No obscure niches of the Word ever once say that God promises to work all things for the good of those who do not love Him (Rom 8:28).

None the less God knows all about us, in a thorough way, from the very beginning; hence He can act in ways that will make His plan and purposes come to pass. He is sovereign in who He picks and assigns as His vessels to carry out what He so desires. And there are always two kinds of vessels and God does not use them in the same way. But He does use both.

Let's first examine what God tells us on those occasions when He chose those that know Him. We should think of them as the people of faith. Then we will look at those that God chose to use that had no love for God; with a few exceptions most of them opposed God and His people.

> Gn 18:19 -- "For I have chosen (known) him, so that he may command his children and his household after him to keep the way of the Lord by doing righteousness and justice; so that the Lord may bring upon Abraham what He has spoken about him."

> Gn 25:23 -- "The Lord said to her, 'Two nations are in your womb; and two peoples will be separated from your body; and one people shall be stronger than the other; and the older shall serve the younger.'"

> 1 Sam 16:1 -- "Now the Lord said to Samuel, 'How long will you grieve over Saul, since I have rejected him from being king over Israel? Fill your horn with oil and go; I will send you to Jesse the Bethlehemite, for I have selected a king for Myself among his sons.'"

Jer 1:5 -- "Before I formed you in the womb I knew you, and before you were born I consecrated you; I have appointed you a prophet to the nations."

I would call some of the men above what Paul calls them (Rom 9:23). They are vessels of mercy upon whom God bestows the riches of His mercy and grace; and He shapes their life for His glory in the end. They each played a huge role in the drama of history that spanned the years before Christ. And through such men God gradually unfolded His redemptive plan for all to see and for all to praise Him. But we must have eyes to see and ears to hear. For without an open heart, willing to believe, there will be nothing but twisted and empty words.

In most texts of the OT the Hebrew word for the verb "know" is most often "yada." This word often implies an intimate knowing in the original language of the Bible. Hence God knew Abraham and God knew Jeremiah; and He called them to His service. Scripture does not say what God knew. But what He knew seems instrumental in His call on their life.

If we can assume that God would know from the very start that a person would believe Him then certainly God can choose for His service or purpose prior to birth. There is no evidence in any of these passages that God caused what He knew. God knows us in an intimate and detailed way.

This may be the same kind of foreknowing that predestined people to believe Christ as was discussed in the last chapter. God foreknew that these people truly believed Him. But God could not have chosen these people in the OT on the basis of their faith in Christ. That faith was still hidden, and was later to be made known. All they had was the promise of One to come, and of course God would give all that truly believed Him that promise.

But they could only claim that promise if they believed God. One might even say that OT saints were predestined to believe

God's promise since they believed God. And certainly if they did not believe God they would not hold to His promise that He would save His people. God would not allow them to understand what He was going to do in and through the One He sent. We must truly believe God if we are going to understand what He is doing and why the cross was necessary. We must live by faith in God, not by faith in our own works.

God Chooses the Nations to Serve Him

God also has His purpose for certain groups of people. He chose one small group to become the nation through which He would carry out His plan for the ages. His design for that nation was to prepare the way for what was to come. They were chosen to keep the oracles of God (Rom 3:2), to speak for God to the rest of the world, and Christ was to come through them (Rom 9:5). God also chose them to fulfill a covenant that He had made with those who had gone before.

> Dt 7:6-10 -- "For you are a holy people to the Lord your God; the Lord your God has chosen you to be a people for His own possession out of all the peoples who are on the face of the earth. The Lord did not set His love on you nor choose you because you were more in number than any of the peoples, for you were the fewest of all peoples, but because the Lord loved you and kept the oath which He swore to your forefathers, the Lord brought you out by a mighty hand and redeemed you from the house of slavery, from the hand of Pharaoh king of Egypt."

Yet the Word of the OT shouts with a thunderous silence; not one of that nation is said to have been given faith in God. No doubt many among them did believe God, and surely God foreknew those that would. As a people they had a rich heritage and a great body of truth about God and His plan, more than all other peoples of the world in their day. Still, only the children of the promise (Rm 9:8), those who believed God, were truly His.

We should not omit here that God shapes the rise and fall of every nation on earth, not just Israel. In the book of Jeremiah we find that God is portrayed as the potter; He acts on the kind of material that He finds in each nation and He makes of that group of people what He so desires. In this way He works out His will for what takes place among the nations (Jer 18). And by His sovereign and wise rule He selects the leaders and numbers their day in the sun.

God Chooses Those with No Faith for His Purposes

Most people in the OT had no love for God and many of them stood contrary to God's people and God's plan. The Word says that God used some of these that had no faith for His purpose too. Yet how He used them was never the same as His plan for those who loved Him.

There is a great gulf fixed between the two that cannot be bridged, other than that God works out His will. And Paul said that those without faith in God are vessels prepared for destruction (Rm 9:22). God restrained His wrath toward their sin for a season so that He could make known His riches on vessels of mercy. God endures those without faith, but He can also use them for His own ends.

One purpose for which God used those who opposed Him was to demonstrate His power and might over them. He wants all to know that He can work out His will despite any and all obstacles thrown up against Him. And from such times we honor and fear Him and people proclaim His name across the earth, for He is Lord of all.

These amazing and dynamic manifestations of His supreme power took place when those who did not know God rose up to oppose what God was doing in and through His own. God does no injustice when He has warned of the coming fate through word and deed; yet the doomed refuse to listen and go on to defy. God knows if they will persist in doing so.

Such was the case with the Pharaoh of Egypt at the time of Moses. And God raised Pharaoh up to enhance His name as He hardened his heart to bring about His will. This only came from God after Pharaoh had shut the door of his own heart (cf. Ex 8:32).

Ex 9:12-17 -- "And the Lord hardened Pharaoh's heart, and he did not listen to them, just as the Lord had spoken to Moses. Then the Lord said to Moses, "Rise up early in the morning and stand before Pharaoh and say to him, 'Thus says the Lord, the God of the Hebrews, Let My people go, that they may serve Me. For this time I will send all My plagues on you and your servants and your people, so that you may know that there is no one like Me in all the earth. For if by now I had put forth My hand struck you and your people with pestilence, you would then have been cut off from the earth. But, indeed, for this reason I have allowed you to remain, in order to show you My power and in order to proclaim My name through all the earth. Still you exalt yourself against My people by not letting them go.'"

God had a second purpose in mind when He chose a proud and sinful man by the name of Nebuchadnezzar and his empire of Babylon. God called this man of idol worship His "servant;" one that He would use to judge and destroy the Holy City in the land of Judah. For the nation chosen of God had drifted from Him; false worship, false gods, their pride, and many other repulsive sins consumed them. No plan of redemption would come through them for the way they were headed. God knew they would not return to Him unless He took action.

Jer 25:8-9 – "Therefore thus says the Lord of hosts, 'Because you have not obeyed My words, behold, I will send and take all the families of the north,' declares the Lord, 'and I will send to Nebuchadnezzar king of Babylon, My servant and will bring them against this land and against its inhabitants and against all these nations round about; and I will utterly destroy them and make them a horror and a hissing, and an everlasting desolation.'"

Later this king of the most vast and powerful empire up until that day gave a testimony to the Lord. He honored God with sound and lofty words that if meant from the heart might declare that He came to know God. Some day we will find out if this man was for real. The fact that his testimony is found in Scripture suggests that he may be.

Dn 4:34-35 -- "But at the end of that period, I, Nebuchadnezzar, raised my eyes toward heaven and my reason returned to me, and I blessed the Most High and praised and honored Him who lives forever; for His dominion is an everlasting dominion, and His kingdom endures from generation to generation. All the inhabitants of the earth are accounted as nothing, but He does according to His will in the host of heaven and among the inhabitants of earth; and no one can ward off His hand or say to Him, 'What have You done?'"

A third way that God used those of wicked living was to show forth His wrath on sin. Through this means God reveals that He is indeed righteous and just; for God tolerates sin only so long. By the demise of wicked people He gives ample warning to all who come after; Sodom and Gomorrah are prime illustrations. The ruins of Jerusalem at the hands of the Chaldeans served as a witness for this end too.

> Jer 22:8-9 -- "Many nations will pass by this city; and they will say to one another, 'Why has the Lord done thus to this great city?' Then they will answer, 'Because they forsook the covenant of the Lord their God and bowed down to other gods and served them.'"

A fourth way that God uses those who do not know Him is to work things for the good of those that do love Him. Hence we should never be surprised at what God does in the pages of our lives or in the course of history. Things that seem hopeless and gut wrenching to us have His permission; yet He will only allow what we can handle with His help.

He sees the end, the beginning, and all that is in between. And if need be God can turn the heart of those who do not know Him toward helping His own. See just one instance in the case of Cyrus, king of Persia (Ezra 1:1-3). The prediction about this man was spoken over 150 years before he came on the scene (Is 45:1-7).

In contrast God never says that He works for the good of those who do not love Him. This obviously would be contrary to His character and His Word. However, those who oppose Him may see what He does and begin to reconsider their plight before Him. And God will respond to them in a patient and inviting way. He wants people to believe Him and love Him. He wants us to know that we must depend solely on His mercy, for our sin separates us from Him and we cannot go to Him except through His Son's death on the cross, for he paid the ransom to set us free from sin and death. God seeks those who will worship Him in Spirit and in truth.

Purpose in Redemption

We could go on to cite many instances from the sea of OT events to show that God has a purpose in all things. Of course the one dominant aim that runs through the OT was to bring about the redemption of those who believe. Most themes and much prophecy pointed toward the day when His Son would enter the world to do the work of the Lamb of God.

All that took place in the OT marched to the beat of God's will and moved toward the day of the cross. And God was always advancing that plan so that the incarnation would come to pass in the fullness of time (Gal 4:4). To do this He protected and shaped the world and His people until all was arranged in good order.

And He knew from the beginning of a yet future epoch beyond the first coming of Christ. And now God works toward that end too. Before that day comes His will is to reach all corners of the earth with the message of His Gospel. When the last day comes there will be those from every tribe and nation who will believe in the One God sent (Rv 5:9).

God's Sovereignty and Man's Belief

But there is a perplexing matter that I still must address. If God has granted that all people are free agents in the matter of belief in Him, then how does God make certain that His will prevails; that all comes to pass as He has said it will? If God values man's free choice, and yet desires to work out His full plan in human history, then we should see in the Bible history that God protects man's free choice. How does He do this while yet being able to accomplish His will overall? For God knows the beginning and the end, and the end will happen just as He has said it will.

Is anything too difficult for God? Can He cause to happen all that He intends yet not compromise our status as free agents who believe of our free will? I have no hesitance in saying an enthused yes. Still, no Scripture fully confirms this to be so. Yet, there is a plethora of Scriptures to show that prophecy is true; and there are more than enough Scriptures that tell us that we must choose to believe. Absent a clear word to the contrary we must believe, or we will die in our sins.

OT writers have left us the premier chronicle of history that shows how God takes those who say "yes" to Him and makes them stand strong and valiantly, against all odds. Then others see Who God is through their witness and come to true faith in Him too. God has always preserved a remnant for His name. They are small in number but great in faith and in the demonstration of God's rule, power, and might. And their witness rings loud and clear, as all those that compete for the hearts of men have once again been vanquished by the arm of the Lord. And those who stay on the wrong side go to meet their fate.

The remnants are those who have lived during the perilous days of history when God dealt with those who refused to listen to Him. God destroys the dregs of those who oppose Him; those who would dare stand in the strength of human and/or evil power and contest His work. Simultaneously God strengthens the remnant with His Word and might, for God will show Who is in charge. He guards their days so that their numbers do not dwindle below what He needs to carry on His plan. And the few will always triumph to the glory of God.

God's purpose for the remnants of history is to preserve faith alive and well. In this way God protects the contingency of Man's free choice to believe. For God knows what to do with the remnants of life. Through the remnants He brings amazing glory to Himself.

God used complex events to guide and protect His own; then the faithful would grow from a few to many. With this in mind, read the story of Joseph and his brothers (Gn 37:18-30). With a thirst for blood in their hearts, the brothers plot to kill the favored one of dad, until the oldest stopped the evil plan.

So the clan of traitors cast Joseph into a pit while they cooked up some nefarious scheme to get rid of him. By God's providence, at that juncture of time and place a caravan of traders just happened by, on their way to Egypt. So the treacherous kinsmen sold him to be a slave. Yet despite what they did Joseph said years later that God meant it for their good. But why?

> Gn 45:5, 6-8 -- "Now do not be grieved or angry with yourselves, because you sold me here, for God sent me before you to preserve life" ... "God sent me before you to preserve for you a remnant in the earth, and to keep you alive by a great deliverance. Now, therefore, it was not you who sent me here, but God; and He has made me a father to Pharaoh and Lord of all his household and ruler over all the land of Egypt."

I doubt that God caused the brothers to sin; rather He shaped the events so that they would sin in a certain way. He prevented what they really wanted to do, which was to kill Joseph (Gn 37:20). And in the end He used the whole episode for the good of those who were His, and for His master plan to work through a nation to bring about the redemption of man. He preserved and grew the remnant. And God used His power through Joseph to teach the whole of them great things about Himself.

Some see the remnants of the Bible as showing that God chooses a few to be saved. This is true, but God does not give them faith, rather He aligns the course of events so that faith endures to be passed on. This is the purpose of the remnants of Scripture; and God only allows the number in the remnant to get so few. Then He takes action; He does what needs to be done to carry His plan forward to a new generation who will respond in faith, and for what He wills to happen.

Yes, we are susceptible to doubt, just like Elijah when he thought he was the only one left alive to serve God (1 Kgs 19:14). But God informed him that there were more than he knew; for God had kept 7000 who had not bowed to the false god of Baal. God knows the number of the remnant.

So how does God work through the remnant? From history we see that He destroys the wicked and keeps, inspires, and empowers those who trust Him. And while He does this He works mightily in that remnant to advance His will; through their witness others come to believe. It is hard to ignore God when the wicked are gone and people can see the work of God in those who serve him faithfully. He displays His power in an extraordinary way in times like these.

Let's look at two more illustrations of this pattern in the OT.

In Jeremiah's day, and the years thereafter, God took a handful of exiles that had faith in Him and guarded their lives against all odds. He kept those who had the spiritual breath of life in them until such time that others would see and listen. God proved His power and might in that small group taken to Babylon in the likes of Daniel, Ezekiel, Shadrach, Meshach, and Abednego. Must we doubt that God will make those of faith stand? Then their prophecy and witness will bear the fruit that God intends; they will grow into a body devoted to Him and kept to forward His cause.

God will accomplish and complete what He intends through those who have faith in Him. He does not infringe on man's free choice to believe, but He can make those men stand who have firm faith until faith is produced in those who follow in their footsteps. There is nothing impossible for God.

A second illustration adds still more weight to this point of view. God does not need a thousand or a few hundred people; God can do the impossible with one man, and his family. How can we be certain of this you might ask?

God did so in the past. God kept a man alive for 950 years to make certain that faith in God was passed on. God took Noah through an earth destroying cataclysmic venture that preserved faith and man as a free agent who can respond. And God did this despite the sin of this man after the flood. Can we imagine the faith of his family and descendents after seeing how God had kept them from destruction? Wouldn't we believe the One Who could and would do that? And would we not fear the God who would destroy all but the one who walks with God.

God does not need many; one man will do. And God by His authority and power will shield that man against all harm, and sustain him against all who oppose. By His sovereign pledge of things to come, He shapes the events that permit the baton of faith to be passed on to others.

All the while God showed his wrath toward sin and those who refused to walk with Him. And the following verses certainly do not read like He controlled the way Man had turned to wickedness.

> Gn 6:5-7 -- "Then the Lord saw that the wickedness of man was great on the earth, and that every intent of the thoughts of his heart was only evil continually. The Lord was sorry that He had made man on the earth, and He was grieved in His Heart. The Lord said, 'I will blot out man whom I have created from the face of the land, from man to animals to creeping things and to birds of the sky; for I am sorry that I have made them.'"

How we read these verses does pose a few problems. The words describe God's reaction as if He didn't know what was going to take place. Yet, since He is omniscient we can be certain that He did know that this was coming from the very start, even before He gave Man the one choice in the garden. But He already had a plan for what He would do when all but one would reject Him. And He too had a plan for the redemption of all who would believe (Gn 3:15); this was to come later; but His plan was in place before He spoke the earth into existence.

We don't know much about the next years after the flood. The Word does not give many details; but God told Noah and his family to populate the world. He lived another 350 years as a living witness to those who came after. Shem, one of his sons, lived 502 years after the flood. Would not their lives testify in a wonderful way to what God will do for those who follow Him? God did not and will not permit true faith to perish from the earth?

But the Word is clear that the people began to drift once again unto the days of the tower of Babel. Then God intervened once again. But the full story of those days is somewhat vague in the Scriptures. Yet no doubt there was a remnant that God used.

Yes, God can take His people and preserve the volition of trust in Him. Or God can permit the numbers to dwindle to just a few and then He will start over with that few. God has done these things in the past. He has done so with neither the message dimming nor His plan being thwarted and perishing from existence.

God will not allow the wickedness of Man to overtake and defeat those who are few in number. God's Word will endure and His plan will unfold. And yes, God will demonstrate His power and might at those times, more than at other times. He will make those of faith stand and not falter, to be His strength.

God constantly seeks people to come to Him. And yes He can reveal Himself to some more than others, for He knows who will respond and who will not, for He knows the heart. He found a heart to respond in Abraham. Yet Abraham was not alone in faith, as there was the priest Melchizedek; and where did he come from?

God is not frustrated by what seems impossible. He can and does work His will through our choice to believe Him. And to refuse to believe will not thwart His will in the march of His plan for the ages.

During one of those fateful past eras when God sorted the sheep from the goats, one of His servants spoke about what God was doing.

Ezek 18:23 -- "Do I have any pleasure in the death of the wicked," declares the Lord God, "rather than that he should turn from his ways and live?"

Ezek 18:32 -- "For I have no pleasure in the death of anyone who dies," declares the Lord God. "Therefore, repent and live."

Ezek 33:11 -- "Say to them, 'As I live!' declares the Lord God, 'I take no pleasure in the death of the wicked, but rather that the wicked turn from his way and live. Turn back, turn back from your evil ways! Why then will you die, O house of Israel?'"

Ezekiel wrote these things in the midst of God's judgment on Judah and Jerusalem, about 587 BC. Does this sound like a God who has a secret will to select just a few? Absolutely not! Rather these words are crystal clear in that God is patient and endures the lost, seeking to save those who would turn to Him. But He will not endure forever. God knows how long He can wait and He will do so.

God is patient, wanting people to turn to Him, while knowing who will and who won't. And God gives them all the opportunity to do so. He reaches out over and over to those who just need to take the time to listen and believe.

> Jer 25:4 -- "And the Lord has sent to you all His servants the prophets again and again, but you have not listened nor inclined your ear to hear."

When the Day of Judgment arrives no one will come before God and accuse Him and say, "You made me not accept You," or "You did not love me." As Paul tells Timothy:

> 1 Tm 2:4 -- "(God) desires all men to be saved and to come to the knowledge of the truth."

And Peter wrote:

> 2 Pt 3:8-9 -- "But do not let this one fact escape your notice, beloved, that with the Lord one day is like a thousand years, and a thousand years like one day. The Lord is not slow about His promise, as some count slowness, but is patient toward you, not wishing for any to perish but for all to come to repentance."

There comes an hour when God will end His wait for those who do not turn; and He knows they will not. He acts in judgment, and I think He did so in the days of the OT to protect His master plan of saving the lost. He honors the volitional response of faith and He will exalt His name through the lives of those who remain. Is it any wonder that other than during the days of Christ, the remnants down through the years have shown forth God's greatest power and revelation in their renewal?

John Piper (2000) in his book the "Pleasures of God" states that since not all people are saved, we have to decide whether we believe that God's will to save all people is restrained by his commitment to human choice, or whether we believe that God's will to save all people is restrained by His commitment to the glorification of His sovereign grace (Eph 1:6, 12, 14, Rom 9:22-23). Piper goes on to say that he does not find in the Bible that people have the ultimate power of self-determination.

I agree in part that here is where the rubber meets the road. But I do not think that what Piper says is an either/or situation. Can it not be both? Is anything too difficult for God? Can He not work out His will to His glory while granting Man a choice to believe or not to believe? Nevertheless God is the one who seeks Man. And God knows who will believe and who will not, and He knows this from the beginning.

Yet we do not determine our own end, because salvation does not come by the works of man, but by what God has done in Christ. Even believing God is not enough; rather God gives salvation in His Son to those that believe Him. Man never earns salvation; it is God's gift. The question is, "To whom does God give His gift? And Abraham believed God and claimed His promise of One to come.

God's will reigns, played out on the world's stage through two groups of people, those who believe God and those who do not? Those who do not are vessels of wrath prepared for destruction. Those with faith in God are vessels of mercy prepared for glory (Rom 9:22-23). Both groups are known from the beginning because God foreknows those who are His. He knows them first by their believing Him, not by their faith in His Son.

He chooses those who believe Him to receive mercy and grace through His Son. For if you truly believe God you are certain to believe in the Son of God. He has chosen us to do so even before we did anything good or bad, and He remembers our sin no more. He treats us as if we have forever been righteous, because we are in Christ.

But those who are vessels of wrath, He loved them with a priceless self-sacrificing love. But they either reject God totally, or they seek some other means to be saved, for many think they please God with their own good works. They never gave God the chance to choose them in Christ, for they refused to believe that God tells us to put our faith in His Son, the One He sent to the cross on our behalf. And when they do not know the Father they will never know the Son. And likewise, if they never believe the Son they clearly do not know the Father.

By the time God wielded His wrath on the OT Hebrew people in the day of Assyria, and then later with Babylon, He had sent His prophets over and over. But the people did not and would not hear them. God, of course, knew that they would not do so since He knows all things. But He was blameless for their rejection of Him. He was patient and gave them many opportunities to repent and turn to Him.

One only needs to study Jeremiah and how this prophet spoke God's Word for over 40 years. Only then did the final day of destruction for the Holy City come; yet God promised a new song, a new heart, and a new day to dawn. These would come through the protected small group in exile; the remnant empowered by God in a very special way. What a witness they were, and are!

Troublesome Passages in the OT

I would like to take a close look at two texts that are troublesome. We find these passages in both the OT and NT. Let me quote:

Is 53:1 -- "Who has believed our message? And to whom has the arm of the Lord been revealed?"

Is 6:8-10 -- "Then I heard the voice of the Lord, saying, "Whom shall I send, and who will go for Us?" Then I said, "Here am I. Send Me!" He said, "Go, and tell this people: 'Keep on listening, but do not perceive; keep on looking, but do not understand. Render the hearts of this people insensitive, their ears dull and their eyes dim, otherwise they might see with their eyes, hear with their ears, understand with their hearts and return and be healed.""

Some of these words, also quoted in the NT (Mt 13:14-15; Mk 4:12; Lk 8:10; Jn 12:40), have been a puzzle to those who would hold that faith in God is a matter of a free will decision.

If we study the passages in the NT carefully we find that those on the outside receive parables, but to those on the inside were granted to understand the mystery of the kingdom of God (Mk 4:11; Mt 13:11). If we truly need to believe God before we can recognize Who the Son is then is it any wonder that God would blind those who are not His? Salvation, faith in Christ, is for none except those who truly believe God.

Also we know that words like these in Scripture can also serve as goads to get people to stop and think. Can we really believe the Word of God and His message if we do not really believe God? Do we really listen to what God says, or do we hear what we want to hear.

Another such goad is "Vanity of vanity, all is vanity" (Eccl 1:2). To those on the outside these words are to prod them to think on what life is all about. Without God all is vanity. And likewise if we do not believe God we will not hear or listen to what He says. Believing God comes prior to hearing what He says.

People must have an open heart to receive the truth, and there are many things in a person's life that interfere with hearing God's voice. Are we consumed or distracted by the empty things of life? Do we really believe God?

But there will also be hearts with good soil (Mk 4:3-20) where what God says can take root. God's message is for those who are downtrodden, sinful, and recognize their need for a savior. They are more likely to believe God and His plan of salvation, for this is our only hope.

Hence, the wise of the world, and the intelligent, and the rich, and the proud do not often come to God. Rather those of faith who come as a child are those who will receive sight, learn of God, and see Christ for Who He is. If we are willing to trust God, rich or poor, wise or ignorant, we will hear His Word through His messengers and we will put our faith in Christ.

So the words of Isaiah in these texts can serve as a goad to those who will not listen. Such words should cause us to stop and think, "Am I listening." Do I hear the truth?" And God does use goads to get people to wonder why they do not understand (Eccl 12:11). And goads are hard to kick against, as Paul discovered (Acts 26:14).

No one will be handed over to the Son except those who believe God, hear God's witness to His Son and heed what He says. These are the ones who believe God like a child and they are predestined to have faith in the Son for salvation. And God will blind all those who try to gain salvation in some other way; for Christ is the righteousness for all that believe. Those that believe God are His elect and they will hear what He says. They have learned from Him and they will believe the Son too.

Summary of Faith in the Old Testament

OT saints believed God and He gave them the promise of
One to come. Abraham believed God; and God deemed this man
as righteous. This is fundamental to both OT and NT thought.
Unless we grasp this basic fact we can end up with some peculiar
thinking about God the Father and God the Son.

Nowhere in the OT is there a statement that says God causes
us to believe Him. But there are many passages in the OT that
speak to Man trusting God and loving Him. God desired that
Man respond to Him and walk with Him. By believing God the
OT saints received and had faith in the promise that God made to
them about the One to come.

None the less, belief or no belief, God rules over the affairs
of Man. He works out His plan for the ages: He does so while
shaping two kinds of vessels, those of faith and those without.
He knows both vessels from the very beginning and uses each
for His purposes. But there is a major distinction in how God
uses the two kinds of vessels. Some are prepared for mercy,
grace, and glory; while others are prepared for destruction.

And no matter how few those of faith became, He
accomplished His will through them. He has protected and
empowered the remnants of history. He has worked with them
in such a way that faith has never failed to pass from one
generation to the next.

Chapter Eight

Faith to Faith

Perhaps the most vital doctrine in the NT is the Deity of Christ; God the Father and Christ are One (Jn 10:30). Even so, Christ taught that we are to believe both God, the One Who sent the Son, and the Son of God. The Scriptural sequence is God, and then Son of God. We cannot come to the Son unless we believe God. He the Father, draws us and gives us to the Son (Jn 5:24; 6:37, 44-45; 17:2-8). God the Father has turned all that belong to Him over to the Son (Mt 11:27; Lk 10:22; Jn 3:35).

God will lose no one that has true faith in Him. He has chosen all that believe Him to have faith in the Son to be saved (Rom 4:24-5:2, 8:28-30; 1 Jn 5:1-10). Eternal life is to know both God and Jesus Christ; the One Who was sent (Jn 17:3). If we do not put our faith in Christ we do not believe God. We have made Him a liar (1 Jn 5:9-10). The Scriptures declare that we are born again by God's will (Jn 1:13). We that truly believe God do His will, which is to place our faith in Christ, the One Whom He sent. Faith in Christ and His work on the cross confirms that God has given us to Him. And God takes great pleasure in adopting us as His children (Jn 1:12; Eph 1:5). By faith in Christ we verify that we truly believe God, the One Who raised Jesus our Lord from the grave; hence we believe God through faith in the Son (1 Pt 1:21).

God knows from the beginning all those that believe Him, and He chose those that do to have faith in Christ for salvation. God does not justify anyone who does not yield to the truth of His Word. God foreknew us, in that we believed Him, the One Who raised Jesus from the dead, the same One that justifies (Rom 4:5; 4:23-24; 8:28-33). And God justifies us and declares us forever righteous and innocent of all sin when we place our faith in Jesus (Rom 3:26), as He has told us to do (1 Jn 5:9-12).

God not only did the work on the cross through and in His Son (1 Cor 5:21); but He also sends His servants to proclaim the good news that He has for the world. He calls those that believe Him with His testimony to the Son (1 Cor 1:9, 2:1-2). And all that listen to and heed His witness will put their faith in Christ to be saved and given eternal life (1 Jn 5:9-11). God indeed does a mighty work in those who believe (Eph 1:17-19). He gives His Son to us, we who believe God; and He gives us to His Son.

The "elect" are those who believe the One Who justifies; we know that He (Rom 4:5, 8:30-33) sent His only Son and raised Him from the dead (Rom 4:23-24). We learn from the Word and from the Spirit's work in our hearts. We acknowledge that we are lost in sin, alienated from Him and at His mercy. From the Word, spoken or written, we know that we can never do even one thing by the works of our hand to gain God's favor. God has said that He accepts nothing but the perfect and pure Lamb that He sent to die in our place. Hence the elect heed the call of God to believe in the Son and His cross work. He is the one and only answer to our sin problem that alienates us from God.

The NT has not changed the fact, known in the OT, that true faith begins with what we think of God. We must first see God for Who He is before we will even realize who we are in our lost and sinful state before Him. Unless we have a true picture of God in His perfect righteousness we will never see the reason or need for the cross. If we don't believe the One Who sent the Son how would we ever come to faith in the One He sent? If we don't believe God how will we ever know the need to believe the Lamb, the One promised by God?

God loves the world and He sent His Son. He grants abundant and amazing mercy and grace. Do we not need to believe His witness to Christ (Mt 3:17; Mk 1:11; Lk 3:22; Jn 5:37, 8:18; 1 Jn 5:9-10; 1 Cor 2:1-2)? He has said that He will declare us righteous, which is not by works of the Law, but rather by faith in Christ (Phil 3:9).

The righteousness of God is revealed to us from faith to faith (Rom 1:17). Faith in Christ depends on whether we truly heed the witness of God to us (1 Jn 5:9-11). And He delivers His witness to us through His Word and by His Spirit. Only those who believe God heed His call to come to Christ. But a person that rejects Christ also rejects the One that calls, the same One that sent Him (Lk 10:16, Jn 13:20). They do not believe God for they have made Him a liar (1 Jn 5:10).

Let's now go to a parable about the elect, those who are chosen, and see if that parable speaks to what has been said up to this point.

Mt 22:1-14 -- "Jesus spoke to them again in parables, saying, "The kingdom of heaven may be compared to a king who gave a wedding feast for his son. And he sent out his slaves to call those who had been invited to the wedding feast, and they were unwilling to come.

Again he sent out other slaves saying, 'Tell those who
have been invited, "Behold, I have prepared my dinner;
my oxen and my fattened livestock are all butchered
and everything is ready; come to the wedding feast."'
But they paid no attention and went their way, one to
his own farm, another to his business, and the rest
seized his slaves and mistreated them and killed them.
But the king was enraged, and he sent his armies and
destroyed those murderers and set their city on fire.
Then he said to His slaves, 'The wedding is ready, but
those who were invited were not worthy. Go therefore
to the main highways, and as many as you find there,
invite to the wedding feast.' Those slaves went out
into the streets, and gathered together all they found,
both evil and good; and the wedding hall was filled
with dinner guests. But when the king came into look
over the dinner guests, he saw a man there who was
not dressed in wedding clothes, and he said to him,
'Friend, how did you come in here without wedding
clothes?' And he was speechless. Then the king said
to the servants, 'Bind him hand and foot, and throw
him into the outer darkness; in that place there will be
weeping and gnashing of teeth.' For many are called,
but few are chosen."

Masters of God's Word have gone back and forth endlessly,
and often fruitlessly, about what Christ taught in this parable.
The question is always, what did He have in mind by the last
sentence? Who are the chosen, known as God's elect in other
places in the NT? Over the years there has been a medley of
proposed answers.

Bible scholars agree on a number of things. The king is God
and the bridegroom is Christ. And the slaves or servants are
God's messengers sent to those in the world.

All acknowledge too that the many people that pay no heed
to God's invitation are included among the lost; they too will be

cast out. They simply have no regard, fear, or desire for God, so they ignore the call to the wedding. God certainly does not choose them.

But questions abound with respect to those that show up for the wedding. They were both good and evil; such is stated. All of them are chosen, except one. He was not dressed in wedding clothes. He attends, but still is cast out.

From the "faith to faith" interpretation the one with the wrong clothes may have had a keen interest in religious things, yet did not belong to God. He did not really believe God, or His call; otherwise he would have come dressed for the occasion. He may have had zeal for what he thought was God (Rom 10:1-3); and maybe he wanted to be where the action was. But he did not believe as Abraham did. Hence he would not be chosen or adopted. God will not give salvation to those that do not truly believe Him, for we are called to the Son through the Father (1 Cor 1:9).

Those in the OT could not have faith or confidence in the promise of God if they did not first believe the One that promised. And the One that promised is the same One that calls us, the same One that sent His Son.

God always seeks the lost as He invites and urges, when He sends His Word and His servants. But we still need to respond to and heed what God says. The kind of deeds that a person has done in the past makes no difference. He welcomes and accepts the good and the evil alike. Both must believe the message of the One Who calls. Of course, "good" in this parable refers to our view from the human side, as there is none good but God (Lk 18:19).

We can now gain further insight as to why the ministry of John the Baptist was so critical. A large flock of sheep already existed when Christ came on the stage of planet earth to begin His incarnate work. The sheep knew God, rather God knew them; and they waited for the Shepherd. And since Christ and God the Father are One, Christ does not shepherd any sheep except those that belong to God. Since they had heard and learned from the Father (Jn 6:45) they would hear Christ's voice, believe Him too, and follow Him; He is the One sent by God to lay down His life for the sheep (Jn 10:11). Christ's work is for those who believe the One Who sent Him (Jn 12:44ff). He and the Father are One. And since they are One there can only be one flock. If we truly believe God then He will make certain that we believe the One He sent in the flesh. We will be born again by His Spirit and by His will.

John the Baptist preached repentance, and turned those who followed him to God. Those baptized by this prophet looked for the soon to come bridegroom, but they had yet to recognize and put their faith in Christ. But they would hear His voice and know Him. As we have seen God the Father gave all that belonged to Him to Christ. There were many who trusted the last OT prophet (Mt 21:23-26; Mk 11:31-32; Lk 20:5-8), hence they believed God; and the priests and elders in the Holy City were fearful of those throngs of people.

So the parable tells us that there is a condition that comes before faith in Christ; we must believe the One Who sent His Son (Jn 5:24). He is the One Who now calls (Rom 8:30) and gives us His witness to the Son. He sends the good news by those who serve Him; and we dare not ignore His servants. We must heed His Word. By God's will those that truly believe Him will put their faith in Christ (Jn 1:13; Rom 3:26, 4:4, 8:27-33). Those who do not believe God cannot come to Christ, for God will not let them. They do not belong to God for they have not learned from Him and they do not know Him. Hence, they will not recognize Christ either, for He is God with us, Immanuel (Is 7:14; Mt 1:23).

"Faith to faith" seems to be the best way to explain the written record in the Scriptures. This pattern seems to hold fast not only for the generation that lived just before and after the cross, but for us today. We first believe the Word, which is God's voice to us, and if we do so we will come to Christ and put our faith in Him. No one can snatch those that belong to God out of His hands, neither the hands of the Father nor of the Son (Jn 10:29).

As we unpack the various texts we must also heed the other witnesses that John names in His Gospel (Jn 5:31-47). They were Moses, the prophets, the OT Scriptures, and the foreseen works of Christ. There were those in that day that had great trust in what these witnesses had to say. And in their trust of what was written and seen they had learned from God. They too would come to faith in Christ (Jn 6:45).

Today we have still more and stronger voices that bear witness. These speak with the authority and power of God: the Word of the NT, what Jesus taught, His works, the cross, the empty tomb, the risen Lord, the Holy Spirit, the OT, the united body of Christ in His Church, the love of saints for each other, and all those of faith who give out the good news. We must believe what God says about His Son through His Word and through His servants. He tells us that victory over sin and death is in Christ. Those who believe will live forever in the presence of God. Those who do not are bound for torment in Hell, banished from God's presence for eternity. They will harden for God will not let them see Christ for Who He is (Rom 11:7-11).

God in His sovereign plan does not let anyone that truly believes Him fail to come to Christ. This would be contrary to His faithfulness and to His Word. God indeed chooses those who believe Him to have the new birth with faith in Christ.

Christ declared that all that truly believe the One Who sent Him have passed out of death into life (Jn 5:24). Of course, we must realize that true belief is more than a cerebral agreement; such faith is a commitment to take Him at His Word, to do what He says. And God has said that the only answer for our sin problem and life after death is found in His Son. We must believe in Christ and that He shed His blood for us. He died for us, in our place, so that we might live forever with Him.

Believing Christ

A potential danger of thinking about salvation in this way is that some might reach the erroneous conclusion that Christ is not One with God the Father. That is not the case, Christ is fully Deity. Yet He also came in the flesh at a planned point in time and space, born of a virgin, and He was fully human. In Him all the fullness of Deity dwells in bodily form (Col 2:9). And He died on the cross, as was foretold in the OT, and He rose again on the third day.

If we deny that He came to this world in the flesh we do not belong to God (1 Jn 4:2). While in the world Christ fulfilled the Law set forth by God through Moses. Though tempted in all manner like us He did not sin (Heb 4:15). He was holy and righteous through and through. The core of our being is desperately wicked; His was totally pure and undefiled, with no hint of blemish (Heb 9:14).

Having lived a righteous life, perfect and free of sin, He became the Lamb of God on our behalf. The cross work of this Lamb was to take away the sin of the world (Jn 1:29). God was in Christ reconciling the world to Himself (2 Cor 5:19). And God declared that these things are true by raising His Son from the dead on the third day, to later ascend to Heaven. And Christ will come again on a yet future day known only to God the Father (Mt 24:36; Mk 13:32).

Christ fulfilled all the functions of a high priest in the Jewish sense, but He did this once and for all (Heb 7:26-28). Christ shed His blood for us. He bore our sin; He died in our place so that we might have a relationship with the Most High. God declares us righteous, those of us who put our faith in the Son.

God justifies us, gives us a new nature; and the Father (Jn 14:26) and the Son (Jn 16:7) send the Holy Spirit to live within us.

But those who refuse to hear the truth of the Word from God reject this High Priest that accomplished a wonderful work for all that truly believe God. Most who think they know God have determined in their minds that they will come to God or bargain with God on their own terms. And why would you want a high priest, or a sacrifice, if you didn't believe God in the first place? Hence, believing the One Who sent the Son must come first.

Christ is the picture of God's perfect love toward us in that while we were yet sinners He died for us (Rom 5:8). By God's sovereign provision of mercy and grace He gives us His Son to break down the barrier between He and us.

Now Christ is mediator between God and Man (1 Tm 2:5); He sits at the right hand of the throne in Heaven (Heb 12:2). Peter declared that God has made Him both Lord and Christ (Acts 2:36). And we believe God through Him (1 Pt 1:21). He is Lord of Lords and King of Kings (Rv 17:14).

We look forward to that day when we will go to be with God in heaven. But we cannot go unless we accept that Christ has paid the death sentence for our sin. God declares us innocent of all sin, when we put our faith in His Son as He has said we must do. As He spoke to Thomas in His last days before the crucifixion:

> Jn 14:4-6 -- "'And you know the way where I am going.' Thomas said to Him, 'Lord, we do not know where You are going, how do we know the way?' Jesus said to him, 'I am the way, and the truth, and the life; no one comes to the Father, but through Me.'"

Believing God, the One Who sent the Son

On the other hand believing God, the One Who sent the Son, is somewhat different than faith in Christ. God the Father is Spirit and we must worship Him in Spirit and in truth (Jn 4:24). He is Holy and can abide no sin in His presence; hence we know that in our sin we are lost without hope. We would be destined for the state of Hell, apart from God in torment for all time.

Nevertheless, God is the One Who loved the world and sent His only Son (Jn 3:16, 5:24). He is the One Who planned the cross (Acts 2:22-24). He is the One Who calls us. He is the One Who has given us the Scriptures. He is the One Who justifies (Rom 4:5). He is the One Who raised Christ from the dead (Rom 5:24; 10:9). He is the One Who chose us in Christ, the sent One, before the foundation of the world (Eph 1:4); and He has adopted us as sons (Eph 1:5). He is the One that has never been seen by human eyes; and He is in blazing, unapproachable light (1 Tm 6:16).

Note that in the last paragraph I listed a number of things about God that we need to know. Most of these are what God does with respect to His Son; and Christ often emphasized the need to believe that God sent the Son (Jn 3:17, 17:3, 8, 21, 23, 25).

God alone knows whether a person truly believes. If we do not we will never come to Christ. If we do believe God He gives us His Son and guides us by His Word and Spirit to have faith in Him. If we truly believe God He makes certain that we accept His Son (1 Jn 5:1-10). On the other hand, when a person refuses to put their faith in Christ they make God a liar; so, they clearly did not, in fact, believe God in the first place.

The full Godhead sent Christ into this world. God chose to do so before the dawn of creation (Mt 25:34; Jn 17:24; Eph 1:4) for He knew Adam was going to fall. And through Christ we have come to know what God the Father is like, for what God the Father does Christ also does (Jn 5:19).

God seems to disclose the Trinity to those that believe Him, those He foreknows. But Christ is only one member of the Trinity and He is doing a very special work of God. This may be why we must first believe God and what we are before Him; only then can we begin to grasp the need for the One Who went to the cross for us.

Such is quite reasonable to what the Scriptures teach as we know that Christ was hidden with God until He came in the flesh (Gal 3:23; Col 1:26-27). Faith in Christ was not known in the OT. When Christ lived amongst us He manifested God to us, so that through His life we come to know more what God is like (Jn 14:7-11). For those who believe, Christ is revealed truth about God.

Those who reject what God has said in His Word, through His servants or through His Son, will without fail reject the Son. They remain in their sin for God will not declare even one person righteous without faith in the Son and His cross work where He paid our debt and cancelled all our sin. And hence the Word states that when we have faith in Christ then God sees us as righteous before Him, clothed in the righteousness of His Son. But this righteousness is not our own (Phil 3:9). Rather this faith in Christ, our salvation, comes from God on the basis of faith. God has done all the work of adopting those that believe Him. He did the work in and through Christ; and He moves us by His Spirit to the new birth with faith in Christ. God's power is great and on display in those that simply believe (Eph 1:19).

Indeed we have become the children of God. He gives us a spiritual birth with faith in Christ (Jn 1:12). Once we belong to Him by faith we have all the promised benefits that accrue as a child of God (Jn 3:16; Eph 1:4ff). Much more, He makes us joint heirs with His Son (Rom 8:17).

And God never fails to complete the work that He begins in the life of those that come to Him (Rom 8:28-30). We can never lose what we have in Christ. God plants us in His Son (Mt 15:13) and there we will be for all future time. No one can snatch us out of the hands of God (Jn 10:28-29).

Believing God's Word

God's Word will bring forth a spiritual birth in us when we believe what He has said to us through those servants that penned His Word. Hence, we can capture the essence of Paul's thoughts on predestination in the eighth chapter of his letter to Rome in a slightly different way. If we truly believe the Word we are sure to put our faith in Christ. God reveals Himself through His Word, and we are called by God to believe His Word. And the end to which God moves us when we believe His Word is toward faith in Christ, which is our salvation. Is this not what Peter wrote?

1 Pt 1:23 – "For you have been born again not of seed which is perishable but imperishable, that is, through the living and enduring word of God."

James, likewise, wrote nearly the same thing. God delivers His will to us through His Word. When we truly believe what He says then we have learned from God; hence we are predestined to faith in Christ. And likewise, if we do not put our faith in Christ we fail to truly believe God's Word. And if we do not believe God's Word we do not believe God for He is the author.

James 1:18 – "In the exercise of His will He brought us forth by the word of truth, so that we would be a kind of first fruits among His creatures."

God also sends His Word by His messengers, those that
know Him. But where there is no Word and no heralds of good
news, there is the world that He made with all that is in it. As
Paul said on Mars Hill the natural order of creation should cause
all to seek God (Acts 17:16-34); though such a search may be
like groping in ignorance. But would the One that knows all fail
to see and respond to such groping? Not on your life, He would
send His Word about His Son through His loyal servants or by
the written text.

The revealing work of God, Father and Son

There remains one work of God the Father and Christ that
yet needs to be thought through to understand our salvation.
This is the work of God revealing Himself to those whom He
chooses. Two passages of Scripture come to mind.

Mt 11:25-27 -- "At that time Jesus said, 'I praise You,
Father, Lord of heaven and earth, that You have hidden
these things from the wise and intelligent and have
revealed them to infants. Yes, Father, for this way was
well-pleasing in Your sight. All things have been
handed over to Me by My Father; and no one knows
the Son, except the Father; nor does anyone know the
Father except the Son, and anyone to whom the Son
wills to reveal (*Him*)." (Parenthesis is not in the
original.)

Lk 10:21-24 -- "At that very time He rejoiced greatly
in the Holy Spirit, and said, 'I praise You, O Father,
Lord of heaven and earth, that You have hidden these
things from the wise and intelligent and have revealed
them to infants. Yes, Father, for this way was well-
pleasing in Your sight. All things have been handed
over to Me by My Father, and no one knows who the
Son is except the Father, and who the Father is except

the Son, and anyone to whom the Son wills to reveal (*Him*)." (Parenthesis is not in the original.)

Obviously these are parallel accounts. They both speak of the Father handing all things over to Christ. We can conclude from these verses that those God gave to Christ were "infants;" and who were these people?

We do not know for certain, but might they be those who trust God, much as a young child trusts their father? They do not come by way of the world's wisdom, by wealth, by rank of position, or by the endowment of a keen mind. And they certainly do not come because they offer good works. Rather they came because they knew they were sinners before a Holy and righteous God. Yet they believed God through the influence of John the Baptist, Moses, the Word of Christ, the OT Scriptures, and the message of the disciples. God called the infants to His Son so that they could be adopted and given life where the Holy Spirit would soon come to dwell.

The designation of the title "infant" leaves little doubt that these people would not nor could not come to Christ on their own. God must do the work since infants are helpless, without proper knowledge, or ability to use what knowledge they might have. And in that pre-cross, pre-NT day how much more would such little ones have been in the dark about what was going on? We have much more light than they, as now the NT is written. God hands the infants over to His Son.

I grant that Christ does not specify any belief in this passage. But if we cannot come to Christ unless we have learned from God (Jn 6:45), then clearly Christ is only being shown to those that believe God. The Father draws them and gives them over to Christ. Christ will be revealed to none but those whom God chooses; those that He knows truly believe Him. They are the infants who have been prepared for faith in Christ. They believed God and He disclosed the Son to them.

The Scriptures also say that Christ reveals the Father though the word for father is not found in the Greek of either passage. So what does Christ reveal? Christ does the same thing the Father does. He seeks the lost just as God the Father does. He also shows us what God is like through His work on the cross. He also reveals that God has a profound love for all sinners, beyond anything we could dream or imagine.

And Christ spoke as One with the Father when He said:

Mt 23:37 -- "Jerusalem, Jerusalem, who kills the prophets and stones those who are sent to her! How often I wanted to gather your children together, the way a hen gathers her chicks under her wings, and you were unwilling."

No one would come to God if He did not take the initiative. He reveals Himself in many ways. God has spoken and "It is written." And the Word became flesh. We must listen and heed.

The voice of God is the one and only source of true life, just as during the days of creation. But if a person only goes part way and makes a feigned claim to believe God, yet they do not put their faith in Christ, then what that person thought they had will be taken away (Mt 13:12; Mk 4:25; Lk 8:18). They have not received the spiritual birth that is willed by God for those who believe Him.

And the most dominant evidence for all to see is the risen Lord (Acts 17:31). Since God raised His Son from the grave the third day, He is both true and He is worthy of all joyous praise. The awesome power of God seen in Christ confirms that what God has said is true (1 Cor 15:1-17). And if Christ is not risen, our faith in Him is futile; we are still in our sin.

Due to the circumstances of any event there will always be those that receive more light than others. This may not seem fair, but God knows the heart, and who will respond to Him. We are responsible for the light we have, and if we respond God will show more about Himself through the Father, Son, or Holy Spirit. But God reserves the right to reveal to whom He will reveal for knowing all things He knows the heart. Only God can be just, merciful, and gracious in how and when He does this.

We never arrive at knowing God through human wisdom or intellect. God always seeks the lost. And when He finds those open to His Word then more will be given (Mt 13:12; Mk 4:25; Lk 8:18). He will take action through the Spirit to fan the glowing embers of belief into a living spiritual soul. They will put their faith in His Son. But we cannot toy with God for He knows the heart. He justifies them by faith in Christ and His work on the cross.

Since God knows all things at all times, He surely knows those who will accept the truth. While yet having a sin nature we can believe God and His Word, but faith in Christ, our salvation, is only given by God's will to those who truly believe Him. If we have come to faith in Christ, God foreknew us by our true belief in Him. He gives us a new nature in Christ.

Yet the Word of truth, all the light that we need, does not always lead to faith in Christ. Most do not believe God. They will not listen to His Word; thus they resist the Holy Spirit (Acts 7:51) and they deny the truth about Christ. And likewise they deny the truth about God that Christ shows to us. Directly before the above verses in Matthew and Luke (Mt 11:20-24; Lk 10:11-16), Christ spoke of two cities that had much light come their way, more than condemned cities prior to that time. He said in graphic terms that they would be found more guilty in the Day of Judgment.

So Christ revealed the truth in those cities; the people simply had no interest in the One that called. They were like those who ignored the king's invitation to the wedding of his son (Mt 22:1-14). Or if by choice they were the vainly pious, they refused to concede that God does not accept the works of their own efforts.

Many in that day, and still now, foolishly think and claim that "good works," or self-flagellation will curry God's favor. Not so, says the Word of truth. We must come to God through faith in His Son (Jn 14:6). And God makes certain that those that believe Him put their faith in the Son with His witness that He gives to those that believe Him.

The Elect of God

A second high risk for this "faith to faith" view is to think that all we must do is to believe the One that sent the Son in order to be saved. This has never been the case. Before Christ came OT saints had to believe God's promise of One to come. Since Christ has come we must now believe in the One that fulfilled that promise, Christ Himself. In either case those that believe God are those who will be saved.

Paul clearly states, that no one can in fact believe the One Who sent the Son without coming to faith in the Son. God has predestined us to do so (Rom 8:28-30), and that before the world was set in place (Eph 1:4). God does a wonderful work in Christ for those that He foreknows. All that think they believe God and yet do not accept Christ do not in fact believe God. He is not their Father.

We know that the new birth comes to us by the Spirit (Jn 3:8). When we truly believe God then His Spirit is free to work within us to convince and convict us of our sin and our need for the Savior. We, in a sense, invite God to do in us what He so desires. And by His Spirit He will use the Word to persuade us to accept Christ. He opens our heart to receive His gift of mercy and grace in His Son.

Salvation is only through the Son of God, the One Who died for us. We never know that we belong to God as His elect until we have faith in Christ. There is no other sure evidence; the new birth seals us in Christ by the Holy Spirit of promise, God's pledge to us (Eph 1:13-14) of more things to come. And this new birth brings forth a new nature in us so that the Holy Spirit can come and not only work in us but to reside in us permanently.

We must always remember that Christ taught that God the Father and He are one. We cannot believe one without faith in the other. But the new birth is to believe in Christ because of what He did on the cross. God was in Christ and was doing the work for His people, those who are the elect. Hence we know more what the Father is like by recognizing Who Christ is.

If we never see that they are One, we fail to know both (Jn 8:19). If someone should happen to think that they believe God and yet they still do not accept Christ, they are not saved. They have no spiritual birth and they are still in their sin. God alone justifies us by giving those that believe Him to Christ.

> Jn 14:7-11 – "If you had known Me, you would have known My Father also; from now on you know Him, and have seen Him.' Philip said to Him, 'Lord, show us the Father, and it is enough for us.' Jesus said to him, 'Have I been so long with you, and yet you have not come to know Me, Philip? He who has seen Me has seen the Father; how can you say, 'Show us the Father?' Do you not believe that I am in the Father, and the Father is in Me? The words that I say to you I do not speak on My own initiative, but the Father abiding in Me does His works. Believe Me that I am in the Father and the Father is in Me; otherwise believe because of the works themselves."

God does not lie. His offer of salvation is genuine to all that wish to come to Him, no matter the depth, breadth, or gravity of their sin. He is no respecter of persons. Anyone can come who will heed His Word. But people will not come if they do not believe what God has said. He does not want any to perish;

rather He is exceedingly patient and wants all to be saved (2 Pt 3:8-9; 1 Tm 2:4).

What does God say? *"He who has the Son has the life; he who does not have the Son of God does not have eternal life* (1 Jn 5:12). The dividing line between eternal life with God and eternal death in Hell resides in faith in the Son of God and His work on the cross.

> 1 Jn 5:9-12 -- "If we receive the testimony of men, the testimony of God is greater; for the testimony of God is this, that He has borne witness concerning His Son. The one who believes in the Son of God has the witness in himself; the one who does not believe God has made Him a liar, because he has not believed in the testimony that God has given concerning His Son. And the testimony is this, that God has given us eternal life, and this life is in His Son. He who has the Son has the life; he who does not have the Son of God does not have the life."

Where does the witness of God come from? First, God uses His Word, but the Scriptures also say that His witness to the Son will be within us (1 Jn 5:7-9). He has resolved this to be so. If we think we have God's Spirit in us, yet not have the Spirit of Christ, we really do not belong to God (Rom 8:9-10). Truly believing God, which means a willingness to do His will, convinces us to place our faith in Christ. By God's choice, those that believe Him will put their full confidence in His Son and His work on the cross for salvation.

As Matthew, Luke, and John say (Mt 11:27; Lk 10:22; Jn 3:35), God the Father has handed all things over to the Son. This does not mean though that we no longer need to believe the One Who sent Christ. To the contrary, John quotes Christ as He said, that eternal life is to know both God and Jesus Christ, the One Whom He sent (Jn 17:3).

One Faith

Now there is one faith. As Peter states:

1 Pt 1:18-21 -- "Knowing that you were not redeemed with perishable things like silver or gold from your futile way of life, inherited from your forefathers, but with precious blood, as of a lamb unblemished and spotless, the blood of Christ. For He was foreknown before the foundation of the world, but has appeared in these last times for the sake of you who through Him are believers in God, who raised Him from the dead and gave Him glory, so that your faith and hope are in God."

When we have faith in Christ this confirms that we have truly believed God's promise, and what He has done for us. In fact Peter said that we now believe God through faith in Christ. When we compare this passage with that of the First Epistle of John quoted above, we find that if we do not believe Christ this shows that we fail to believe God. And if we do not believe God we will never come to faith in God's Son, for they are One.

Faith in One is contingent on faith in the other. The two faiths link together, merge into one faith, at the time of salvation, and the bonding between them cannot be broken. God has established this to be so.

We believe God, just as Abraham did; and God calls us and hands us over to His Son. Faith in Christ is our salvation. But prior to this last faith we must accept that we are lost and a sinner before a Holy and righteous God (Rom 3:23, 6:23). We are alienated from Him and under the penalty of death imposed by God in Eden (Gn 2:17). If we do not listen to God and what He says in His Word, we will not come to Christ. So faith in Christ, being born again, comes by God, by His Word, and by the Holy Spirit. We never arrive at Christ except by God's doing as He works in the hearts of those that believe Him.

Those who seem to believe God or have faith in Christ

Millions through the years and around the world today have claimed, and do claim, to worship the one true God. Yet few come to faith in Christ. We saw this too during the days of incarnation when Christ was with us on earth. Some were, and are, super religious in claim and habit. What about all these people? How can this be?

Paul said that they may not know enough (Rom 10:2). Those who lack the Word of God, written or spoken, do not have the right information. They will never come to understand God's Holy and righteous ways. They will have nothing more than a vague idea of Who Christ is; hence, they will never see the need to put their faith in Him to be saved.

Many explore the Word of God but still never experience a spiritual birth. Some, in fact, read and study the Bible much more than those that have true faith; just as the Scribes and Pharisees did during Christ's days on earth. Why don't they come to Christ? The Word states in no uncertain terms that they do not believe God (1 Jn 5:10). They refuse to submit to what He tells us in His Word. They reject the righteousness that God gives us in Christ (Rom 10:3-5).

They might come close while they reserve a full commitment to what is written. Some say that the Bible contains the truth. Then they pick and choose what they think God meant, as if the Word is a blend of truth and fiction. They wallow in the quagmire of treacherous quicksand; many that sort the Scriptures into what they think is truth and not truth ignore or dismiss God's call on them to come to Christ. And if they do not put their faith in Christ they speak and live as if God lies.

Many are openly "religious" in their daily life, but they are no more than the blind that led the blind during Christ's days on earth. They do not know God, for they do not believe Him, and God does not know them. Hence they will read the Word and not hear it. If someone does not believe God then how can they understand His Word; and His Word tells us how to be saved.

Many have a strong taste and passion for the Law; they read the Bible and think that they must abide by laws and do good works to win God's approval and acceptance. The Word does not say this. To substitute works for God's gift of His Son is to tell God that they will try to attain salvation in their own way. We can never earn our way to heaven. Rather God gives heaven to us when we truly believe Him, for He plants us in Christ. And the way of belief is open to good and evil alike as we noted in the parable about the king that gave a wedding for his son.

When anyone tries to add even a single iota of good works from their own hands they, in a sense, tell God they don't believe Him. They twist what is written to their demise. They reject Christ, or say that what He did is not sufficient; what a blatant insult this is to the cross work of God's Son, and to the One Who sent Him to this world to fulfill His purpose, to save His people from their sin.

And there are organized religious groups (I will not call them churches here) that try to keep control over how they think people attain salvation. They add certain rites or practices that they say we must do in order to be saved or to remain saved. In this they add to or distort the Scriptures, that which God has said. They promote human prescribed rites above the power and sovereignty of God. Not so, says God's Word. God saves those that believe Him, for He is the One Who chooses us in Christ. He alone decides who are His. He is the One that gives us mercy and grace in His Son.

No clergy imposed creed or doctrine can take the place of believing God. And if God does not give a person to Christ that person is not saved no matter the dictates or edicts of a religious body, and no matter the rites of a human revered ceremony. A church or a ritual by a church does not justify. Nor do such rites add or lead to righteousness; rather God is the One Who justifies.

He gives those that believe Him to Christ; they are born again by His will alone. He is the only One that knows the sheep of His pasture, for He searches the heart.

We need to think again if we are absorbed by the thought that some religious practice has helped to save or add to our salvation. Christ's death on the cross paid the full debt for us. God is satisfied with Him alone. He made the full and complete sacrifice for us.

Over the years numbers beyond count have had a zeal for God (Rom 10:2); and in nearly all cases misled minds seek to gain God's favor by human effort. And the most deceptive and vain conceit is to think that if on balance we do more good than bad, then God will accept us (Rom 10:3). He will not; He has said that there is only one way to come. He accepts nothing but the pure and perfect righteousness of Christ.

We cannot add one crumb to what Christ has done. To try to do so defames and profanes the broken body and shed blood of God's Son. Our efforts are futile; any avowed works by our own hands tell God He didn't do enough. He has said that His provision of Christ for us is enough; and there is nothing more.

We will always have tares in the midst of the wheat (Mt 13:24-30), those that God did not plant (Mt 15:13). These are like the one called Judas who lived as one of the twelve. They often have an agenda that falls far short of God's plan. Only God knows those that belong to Him by faith. So there are those whom God has not really given to Christ (Jn 6:65). And we as God's people are to leave the tares with the wheat until the end time when God will sift the harvest (Mt 13:30).

Those that appear on the surface to belong to God are like the falsely pious leaders in Christ's day. They claimed Abraham for their father; they alleged that they were the chosen ones, for they were of Jewish descent. But they held to the Law rather than simply believe God as Abraham did.

As we have seen they had the wrong view of what being chosen was all about. They thought that their natural birth heritage was what caused them to belong to God. We should take care, too, so that we do not fall for a false idea that there is some way of coming to God other than to believe Him. Salvation is by God's doing but only for those who have learned from Him. God is the One who justifies (Rom 4:5). We are in Christ because of God (1 Cor 1:30) for His message to us is how to get right with Him, by faith in His Son.

We can now begin to see why Christ provoked so much opposition and out and out hatred from the Priests, Scribes, and Pharisees of His day. He told them over and over that they had no relationship with God; they didn't know Him. God was not their Father, for if He were they would believe Christ, they would love Him, and they would have been willing to do God's will. They would also be willing to do God's work which was to believe in Christ (Jn 6:29). Rather, these men who were corrupt whitewashed death filled tombs (Mt 23:27), placed their hope in the works of their own hands; they rejected the mercy and grace that God provides in His Son.

We can grasp too why Paul incited so much strife and division in the synagogues on his travels. He told the people that God chose some of them to have faith in Christ. They were the ones that belonged to God. Wouldn't that have stirred a fierce "better than thou fuss" among the super religious, but dead synagogue crowds of that day. Little wonder they wanted to drive Paul out of town or put him to death.

The self-professed worshipers boasted in the pride of keeping the law and their human inspired wisdom. They did not believe as Abraham did that God would provide mercy and grace in His own way. So they refused to put their faith in Christ. They did not know or belong to God, no matter how pious they claimed to be. They did not simply believe what God was doing through and in the One He sent.

Comparing Salvation in the Old and New Testaments

Let me review the basics of salvation from a "faith to faith" point of view for both the OT and the NT. This is to clarify any loose ends or missed thoughts that have been expressed along the way.

OT saints, in the manner of Abraham, believed God Who gave them the promise of One to come (Gn 15:6). Their salvation was certain to happen if they believed God. We cannot claim a promise, if we do not believe the one that makes the promise. And the promise to them was Christ, the One Who was to come at a yet future time.

When we get to the NT we receive salvation by placing our faith in Christ, the promise now fulfilled but given to us who truly believe God. The whole process is through faith. God was in Christ reconciling the world to Himself, and adopting us as His sons (2 Cor 5:18-19). But does God redeem those that do not believe Him?

We must keep in mind that in the day of Christ, and then Paul, people were led by the light of the OT. The central thought in the OT is that the first patriarch believed God the Father and He gave them the promise. Paul and the other NT authors do not change this basic axiom of all the Scriptures (cf Rom 4:20-24). True belief must start with God, what He says about our need before Him and His promise to meet that need. The One He sent fulfilled that promise. God tells those of us that believe Him to put our faith in His Son. Those that believe God will do so.

To add more leverage to this premise let me digress for a moment and ponder once again the role of the high priest in the OT; as Christ is our high priest (Heb 3:1). Did not the high priest offer a sacrifice on the Day of Atonement for those who were the people of God? Such sacrifice would not have been for those who rejected God, those who did not belong to Him, those who did not believe Him.

A. Pink (1930) in his book "The Sovereignty of God" reached the same conclusion. The high priest made the sacrifice for those who belonged to God. Yet Pink missed the point of the Scriptures, such sacrifice was made for those who believed God as Abraham did, not for those who did not know God. And in the same way in the NT, Christ is the high priest for those who believe God, and we are to put our faith in Jesus and His work on the cross. And if we truly believe God He gives us the spiritual birth with faith in Christ. And if we do not believe God He will not let us see Christ for Who He is, God with us.

I wrestle in thought with what took place before the incarnation and how the sacrificial system was a picture of what Christ was going to do. There are few doubts in my mind that a sacrifice, that looked forward to the time of Christ, was futile for those who did not know God. So is not Christ in the role of the Lamb of God? He is doing the work on behalf of God's people, those that truly believe Him. God does not choose His people in an arbitrary manner. He chose those that believe Him. And if God did not choose us He might lose some that truly believe Him along the way. He will lose no one.

Christ came to take away the sin of the world (Jn 1:29). All may come who truly believe God and want a relationship with Him, for the message of the gospel is reconciliation (2 Cor 5:18-21). God has said that when we believe Him we will put our faith in His Son and He will adopt us and declare us righteous, innocent of all sin. He will never again see us as under sin's penalty. We are His children not because of any work on our part, but rather because Christ was indeed righteous and gave His life for us. And God said that this was so by raising Him from the dead. But if we reject Christ we also reject the One that sent Him (Lk 10:16; Jn 12:48) for we do not believe that God has made His Son the cornerstone in His kingdom (Mt 21:33-46; Acts 4:11; 1 Pt 2:6-8).

Is faith in Christ a "free will" decision?

This question can be answered in two distinct ways from a "faith to faith" point of view. But only one can be Biblically correct. Let me discuss the strict "free will" side first, and then propose a second line of thought that seems to fit better with the texts of Scripture.

Strict "Free Will" View

To have total "free will" there must be no constraints on a decision. But the Word tells us that there is a condition placed on our faith in Christ. That constraint is if we truly believe God. We cannot come to Christ in true faith in His work on the cross unless we believe God; for He has said that His mercy and grace are given to us through the One He sent.

So the choice to put our faith in Christ is not fully free, rather the choice is conditional. God, through His Word and by His will, has established the "condition" part of that choice. Yet the choice could still be free. We simply must adhere to the conditions of what this faith means. If we do not receive Christ as our Savior, we make God a liar. We not only reject Christ, we also reject the One Who sent Him (Lk 10:16; Jn 12:44-50).

Let me use an earthly example to explain this first option. Suppose the king of my country tells me that if I believe him then I will trust a representative that he will send to me. I am to put my full confidence in the one he will send. But he also tells me that if I refuse to trust his representative, then I really do not believe him, the king.

Because I do believe the king and what he tells me about the one he sends, I decide to put my trust in this representative. But if I do not believe the king then I surely will not trust his representative. Belief starts with what I think of the king.

In a sense the will of the king imposes a condition for completing my belief in him. That condition is to trust his representative. So when I trust the one he sent I do what the king, whom I believe, wills for me to do.

And in the same manner, since I believe God and what He has said about His Son, I trust in Christ. Hence I do God's will by placing my faith in His Son. And John wrote that we are born again by God's will (Jn 1:13). Also, as a Christian when I believe the Son, this demonstrates that I believe God; the One Who sent the Son and called me to the Son. And as Peter said, I believe God through faith in the Son of God.

In this instance there is one decision to make, but the decision is conditional. God fulfills His OT promise to us, those who believe Him, when we place our faith in Christ?

We must be cautious about such an example. We must not think that Christ is just any kind of representative. Rather, He is one with the One Who sent. He is fully Deity, but He was also fully man and He shed His blood for us. He does the work of fulfilling the purpose that the One Who sent Him planned even before Adam fell in the Garden.

God gives us Salvation

A few Scriptural problems arise with the above strict "free will" view. I can explain these best by looking at a second option. This second proposal seems more convincing when we look at what the texts of the Word say.

The second explanation holds that "faith in Christ," our salvation, is neither of ourselves nor by our will. Rather we come to faith in Christ by God's will. Yet we still have a measure of free will. We must first believe God and His Word.

"Faith in Christ" on the other hand is the spiritual birth that God gives to those that believe Him, the One Who sent Christ. When we truly believe God His Spirit guides us and convinces us that Christ is the answer to our sin problem before God. And we are born again by the power of the Holy Spirit using God's Word which brings forth spiritual life in us.

There are several Scriptural reasons to prefer this second alternative. Let's think first in terms of the OT, as from the background of the authors of all the NT books. To them all things began with God and every good and perfect gift comes from Him. The promise of Christ, the gift of mercy and grace, was made to those who believed God, much as Abraham did. They claimed the promise of the One to come, since they believed God and His Word.

Christ, the second person of the Trinity, and His cross work, is now the promise fulfilled. So God does a work in the lives of those that believe Him, He gives us the new birth, which is salvation, or "faith in Christ." But it does no good to claim a promise unless we have full confidence in the One that makes the promise and gives us His witness. Hence our faith is indeed in God just as Peter said (1 Pt 1:21).

A second line of thought from an OT background is to recognize that faith in Christ was not known before the days of incarnation. Paul clearly taught this in a number of places (Gal 3:23; Col 1:26-27; Rom 16:25-26). Hence, faith in God the Father which was known in the OT comes before faith in the Son.

What is very crucial for the line of reasoning here is that God could not choose anyone for His purpose throughout the OT era based on faith or no faith in Christ. Such faith was not known at that time. Hence God's elect cannot be those who believe Christ. Yet God still chose for His purposes in the OT. Might not His choosing for a purpose in the pre-cross era have been based on His foreknowing that one would truly believe God or not believe in God? If so then why should not the same principle be seen and applied in the NT for salvation.

God's plan even for the OT saints was for them to be justified in Christ just as we are today. As Paul says God chose us in Christ before the foundation of the world (Eph 1:4). Hence OT saints were just as much in Christ as we are in the post-cross era. Because of this certainty, God must do the action of giving salvation. And salvation cannot be a "free will" decision on our part, nor on the part of OT saints who neither had nor knew about that option in the manner that we now know. Yet they were saved just as we are. If they understood their Scriptures they belonged to God because they believed Him as Abraham did, and since they believed Him they claimed His promise of the One to come.

Then there are a number of textual nuggets in the NT that say that adoption by God comes by His will (Jn 1:13). And God chose us in Christ before the earth was formed. And He did so by the kind intention and pleasure of His will (Eph 1:9). The choice seems to be entirely His; and we must keep in mind that we are at His mercy.

His choice of us in Christ is a common theme in the NT. Further, texts state that we are predestined by God Who has a purpose and works all things after the counsel of His will (Eph 1:11). Clearly, God is the One that decides whom He adopts into His family and whom He seals with the Holy Spirit and gives an inheritance.

Who would be better able to discern true belief in the heart than God, and who is better at helping our helpless condition for we do not even know what to ask for (Rom 8:26)? We are mere infants when we believe God and God must do a work to adopt us. He reveals what He has done for us in Christ and calls those that believe Him to His Son. We would not know what to do to be saved if God did not tell us what to do.

Other Scriptures also strengthen this idea. We are planted by God (Mt 15:13; Is 61:3). And John writes that God will lose no one that belongs to Him (Jn 10:28-29).

Can God depend on us and our "wisdom" to end up in Christ? I doubt this to be the case, and this certainly could not have been the case in the post-cross era before the NT was written. Rather God has established that if we believe Him He will justify us in Christ. God chooses us for salvation; the "us" refers to those who believe God. We are indeed secure when we truly believe God.

Paul uses very strong language that the sum total of salvation, that is "faith in Christ," is God's gift to us. The question is to whom does He give this gift?

Those that believe Him and the truth of His Word are the most likely option. They are the best candidates for being the elect of God. In this the Scriptures claim that all who truly believe God will come to Christ. God makes certain that this happens. In this sense God's grace is irresistible, but only for those who truly believe God (cf Phil 3:9). Only those that truly believe the One that sent Christ will recognize and see Christ for Who He is, for they are One.

With whom does God make a covenant? Are they those who reject God, those who do not believe Him? Rather all those who truly believe God fall under the new covenant. His promise is certain for them, for God does all the work of giving mercy and grace to those He knows. He indeed not only allows us to have faith in Christ but predestines us to believe in Christ. Faith in Christ, our salvation, is God's gift to all those that truly believe God.

We see this in the Scriptures when all those who follow John the Baptist come to Christ for we know that they believed God before they came to faith in Christ. And why do some that seem to follow God not come to His Son? Would God fail to guide those that believe Him to the Savior? Is He not the One who gives us mercy and grace? Is He inconsistent? Is He not just? Would God be unfaithful to those that truly believe Him? And when would we see our need of a Savior if we do not first believe God?

Since God the Father and Christ are One they have precisely the same flock of sheep. And Christ is doing a work for His flock of sheep. God's purpose for those who truly believe Him will be completely fulfilled. They will be conformed to the image of His Son, justified, and ultimately glorified (Rom 8:28-30). The certainty is beyond question. Hence "faith in Christ," our salvation, is indeed God's gift to us, those who believe Him and His Word. God is faithful to those that are His elect.

And God chose us out of the pure pleasure of His will (Eph 1:4-5). Belief never makes God indebted toward us. He owes us nothing. His sovereign decision before the dawn of the first day was to save those that believe Him. They are His elect. They claim no works or self-effort to gain God's approval. They come by simple faith and they know that their sin is a total affront to a Holy and righteous God. They know too that belief earns nothing from God as the Scriptures clearly state there is no good work involved (Rom 3:20-28; Eph 2:8-9; 2 Tm 1:9). God simply acts to save us out of His mercy and grace.

A few more thoughts should lead us to pause and ponder. Salvation is certainly not of our doing and not due us or earned by us for believing God. Belief is not a work of righteousness; rather God's mercy comes from Himself. We do not deserve a single thing. Even when we believe the One that sent His Son we remain in our sins, He has not justified us. The choice was His to grant a pardon and give new life in his Son, all from mercy and grace. We are called to Christ through Him.

And there is still more, He gives us so much at the time of faith in Christ. He declares us righteous forever, innocent of all sin done in the past and present, and all the sin we will do in the future. He regenerates us by His Spirit and instills a new nature in us. And He seals us by the Holy Spirit with promise of more to come. These things happen by God's will. Is it any less of a problem to think that salvation, that is "faith in Christ," is a certain gift from Him too? Since all these things happen for those who believe God, they are done at the behest of God's vast resources of both His treasures and His power. He is the One that calls us, and He is the gatekeeper to Christ.

His Word explains the way and as such our union to Christ is secure and cannot be changed nor undone. Salvation is from God; but we must first believe God and His Word.

Such a claim is further implied and supported by the fact that God only reveals Christ to those who believe. So the Gospel will be hid from all those who do not believe. And Paul describes this process in the following verses:

> 2 Cor 4:1-6 -- "Therefore, since we have this ministry, as we received mercy, we do not lose heart, but we have renounced the things hidden because of shame, not walking in craftiness or adulterating the word of God, but by the manifestation of truth commending ourselves to every man's conscience in the sight of God. And even if our gospel is veiled, it is veiled to those who are perishing, in whose case the god of this world has blinded the minds of the unbelieving, that they might not see the light of the gospel of the glory of Christ, who is the image of God. For we do not preach ourselves but Christ Jesus as Lord, and ourselves as your bond-servants for Jesus' sake. For God, who said, 'Light shall shine out of darkness,' is the One who has shone in our hearts to give the Light of the knowledge of the glory of God in the face of Christ."

In this text belief comes before seeing the light of the Gospel. Hence such belief is not just in Christ; rather this belief is before faith in Christ. Does the passage not refer to believing God and His truth? Is it not those who believe God and His truth whom God will save?

God reveals Christ and His salvation truth to those that believe Him. On the other hand Christ will be veiled to those that do not believe. God has shone in our hearts, those that believe, so that we recognize and come to Christ. Those that believe God and His truth will have light and they are the ones who are being saved. Those that perish believe neither God nor the truth of His Word. They are not the elect for they do not believe God, the One that sent His Son.

Since God is doing the revealing of Christ, He is the one who does the work of salvation in our hearts. As Christ said:

> Jn 5:24 -- "Truly, truly, I say to you, he who hears My word, and believes Him who sent Me, has eternal life, and does not come into judgment, but has passed out of death into life."

Those that truly believe God have passed from death to life. God will not lose even one of them; they are predestined for faith in Christ. Salvation indeed is a powerful and creative work of God in those that believe. He gives all that believe Him to the Son.

Due to this certainty we can say that our salvation is secure, not based on our choice of Christ, but rather based on God's choice of us. If we think that we are in Christ solely based on our choice we have it wrong. Those that put their faith in Christ only do so by God's will and purpose in those who are the elect, but the elect are those that believe the God who justifies, the One Who sent the Son and raised Him from the dead (Rom 4:5, 4:24; 8:28-33).

On the other hand believing God is our choice. If we come to God under any guise other than purely believing Him, He will not lift the veil from our eyes to see that Jesus is the answer to our sin problem that alienates us from Him.

Proclaiming the Gospel Today

Now we can proclaim the same message that Christ gave to the clerics of His days on earth. If you reject Christ then God is not your Father, for if He were you would believe in Christ. We cannot believe and know God and still reject Christ. They are One.

Should that not send a frightful warning and a wakeup call? And in like manner, the early Christians provoked intense fury and threats among those that seemed sincere; but they were doomed in their foolish attempts to try and please God. Those of faith at that time suffered loss despite their love for God and His Son. They desired that all would be saved, just as God does (Rom 10:1-2; 2 Pt 3:8-9; 1 Tm 2:4).

God's call to have faith in His Son, His gift to the world, is a genuine offer to all people. The gift of salvation is free to those who will believe the giver of the gift and do the will of God which is to put our faith in the One given. Sadly, most ignore God's testimony to His Son (1 Cor 2:1). But Christ is God's wisdom (1 Cor 1:24). God wants all people to put their faith in Christ for He has sent His servants over and over telling us that God loves us. His Word warns us throughout that our destiny in life and after death depends on what we do with His Son.

One more question perhaps needs to be addressed. Can a person come to true faith in Christ, absent true faith in God? I do not think that this is possible. Why would anyone think it needful to be reconciled to someone that they do not believe or want to know? The spiritual birth is only given to those who will listen and heed God's voice to us. When we believe Christ we do indeed believe God. We accept the cross work as done on our behalf before a Holy and righteous God. God has said to accept His plan of salvation.

We should be concerned about the way many pastors and some evangelists present Christ. Do we dare present the Son in the absence of believing God? If we do so, why would we even think we need a Savior? God, His Spirit, and His Word tell us that we need to be rescued from our sinful state before Him.

Christ is not just a friend we can count on; He is the Redeemer Who bought us with His blood so that we can have a relationship with God Whom we believe sent the Son for this purpose. Christ is not just a good role model to live by; rather He is the Savior from sin's penalty and power over us. And God clothes us in His Son's righteousness, declaring us innocent of all sin. By what Christ did God reconciles us to Himself. Christ's death on the cross broke the barrier that separated us from God.

Some promote being born again as a new start or a new lease on life without a spiritual birth, that which is wrought by God in those who truly believe. Not a few false teachers emphasize some of the worthy things that Christ taught but with no new birth; they promote a social gospel for the poor or down trodden. They fail to understand what God really wants to give us. We must be careful about what we communicate when we tell others about Christ. Some of those who seem to follow Him do not have genuine faith. They are not the children of God.

The sad facts are that most who claim they know God believe neither Him nor His Word. To have an intense zeal for God is no substitute (Rom 10:2). We must guard against a superficial mental nod in His direction; we must commit to and own what He says. If a person does not believe God's Word or His witness to His Son, then that person certainly does not believe the One Who sent the Son. Nor will that person come to faith in Christ, for He and the Father are one.

Then there are people that know very little about God or about the One He sent. We must present God in full measure to these people. They need to know Who He is and what He is like before they can even begin to grasp their need for Christ. They need to understand that God is Creator, perfect and righteous, and that there is a great gulf fixed between He and us due to the Fall of Man and our sin nature. We must understand our lost condition before God, and then and only then will Christ make sense. So faith in Christ can only follow once people truly believe God and what He says.

To reach the cultures of other lands we must guard against proclaiming Christ in a vacuum. If God is the One who saves people, justifies them, then people must first understand basic truths about God. They will see no need to accept Christ unless they believe God. They must be told Who God is, what He is like, what He has said, and that He loves us. If those in a raw culture never believe God and what He has said about His Son they will never see the reason for the crosswork of Christ on their behalf. To think that we can come to Christ without believing the One Who sent Him is sheer folly. Yet this is what some unwittingly teach.

People need to read and hear God's testimony about His Son; this is God's Gospel. They need to know that God loves them despite their sin against Him; and He with sacrificial love sent His Son to lay down His life for them. We must warn them of the perils of rejecting Christ, because if they do so they also reject the One Who sent Him (Lk 10:16); their end is Hell. Torment will be their lot forever (Rv 20:10-15).

Today the people of our culture likewise need pure and unblemished truth about Who God is. We must be alert not to dilute or change, or distort what the Word says about God. While all powerful and all knowing, He also loves the world and wants all to be saved. He wants all to come to His Son for salvation.

We must be careful and not substitute some trite or shallow change in our life for what God desires to do in us. God's Word is meant to bring forth a new birth and transform us. God will only grant us to have faith in His Son when we truly believe the One that sent Him. I doubt very much if we can believe the One Who is God with us if we don't believe God the Father. True faith in God leads to faith in Christ every time.

Ordo Salutis

Let's take our one and only look at the *ordo salutis,* the steps toward salvation spelled out in the Scriptures. We can only see these from the human viewpoint, as God knows all steps simultaneously. There is no time sequence for Him, as He is outside of time. Still, there is a causal sequence. So let's look at the steps.

1. God seeks through His creation, His Word, His messengers, Christ's life, His works, His death and resurrection, and the work of the Holy Spirit.

2. Truly believing God (the One Who justifies, Who sent His Son, and Who raised His Son from the dead, the One Who tolerates no sin in His presence) (becoming one of the elect).

3. Conviction of sin by the Holy Spirit with repentance (Only allowed when one truly believes God, internal witness that Christ is the answer to our sin problem)

4. Faith in Christ (justified, born again, adopted, regenerated by work of Holy Spirit)

5. Sanctification by faith and work of Holy Spirit

6. Glorification upon death

I have no intention or desire at this time to compare the above steps with those that have gone before. Those who care to do the research can take the time to do so.

Revisiting the Five Points of Calvinism

Total Depravity

Many teach that we can do nothing apart from Christ (Jn 15:5). An error most common to all of us who study the texts of Scripture is to interpret a verse out of its context. This specific verse in John has to do with bearing fruit by those that are in the vine. The passage has nothing to do with coming to Christ for salvation in the first place. Do we need to believe the vine dresser before we become one of the branches placed in Christ?

We are lost, total sinners, depraved in all respects until saving faith in Christ. Believing only the One Who sent Christ does not rectify this (cf 1 Jn 5:1-10). We are only born again when we accept Christ.

But is there anything in the Word that says a sinner cannot believe God? Yes, sinners need light, and we know that God seeks and reveals. No one would come to God except by His search for those who might respond. And how do we know we are sinners and in need of a Savior unless we believe God and acknowledge Him for Who He is?

To believe God is our "free will" choice, and open to the worst of sinners. On the other hand saving faith in Christ comes when we truly believe God and the revealed truth of His Word. God's Word used by the Holy Spirit convicts us of our sin and our need for His Son. We are indeed born again in Christ by God's will, for His will for those that believe Him is to put our trust in His Son, the second person of the Trinity. To truly believe God leads to faith in Christ every time.

Despite any concept of "total depravity," if God says we need to believe then all have the capacity to believe. *"God has put eternity in our hearts without which man will not find out the work which God has done from the beginning even to the end"* (Eccl 3:9).

Yet, belief does not save people. Belief is also not a work of righteousness. People are dead and powerless to do anything about their sinful state. But through faith, due to promise, God remedies our lost and sinful state with the shed blood of His Son. He regenerates us and grants us new life in Christ. God does the saving and He promises to do so when we receive His Son.

In all this there seems to be a common grace that allows anyone to believe God and His Word if they are willing. But the new birth is spiritual, willed by God through His Word by the Holy Spirit, for all that believe. Salvation, faith in Christ, is God's gift to the world for all those that believe God.

Unconditional Election

God by the pleasure of His will decided before the dawn of the first day that He would choose all that believe Him and His Word to be in Christ. Unconditional election as taught by strict Calvin scholars does not reflect the truth of what God's Word says. Rather the "elect" are those who believe the One Who justifies, none other than God.

We see this spelled out most clearly in Romans, John, and 1 John. If we truly believe God and what He says about His Son we are certain to put our faith in Christ. Belief always means a willingness to do what the One we believe says to do. If we believe God, the One Who sent His Son, we are predestined by Him to put our faith in Christ. They are One. Only those who truly believe God will see Christ for Who He is.

The process is "faith to faith" as presented by Paul in Romans 1:16-17, but ignored or misunderstood by scholars who study the text of Romans. God's purpose for His elect, those that truly believe Him, is certain. The elect will be justified by faith in Christ, conformed to His image, and glorified in the future.

Limited Atonement

Salvation is available to all people. There is no limited atonement as taught by strict Calvinists. All may come that are willing to believe the truth of what God has said and put their faith in Christ. The atonement is only applied to those who believe God for they will without fail put their faith in Christ.

The concept of limited atonement does not conform to Scripture. Hence this doctrine is not of the Lord and gravely distorts the truth. Christ's death on the cross is sufficient for all. Anyone can become God's elect and respond to God's grace offered in Christ.

On the other hand if we stoop to think that God toys with the mind when He invites people to His Son, then where is truth? If we cannot have complete trust in His promise, then who is God? If we cannot present the Gospel and know that His offer is genuine for all that hear then we partake in the greatest fraud of all.

No, there is too much Scripture that tells us that the invitation from God is genuine. His gift is available to all that will believe Him. God states that He sent His servants again and again, but people would neither yield to nor come to Him.

Salvation is not universal though the atonement is not limited. All can come to Christ who believe that God sent His Son to die in our place. But if we put our faith in Christ without truly believing God, our faith means nothing. How can we have true faith in the Lamb of God before we know that we need the Lamb before a righteous God?

So Christ died for the world and also for the "many" (Mt 1:21, 20:28, 26:28; Heb 9:28). He died for the many, those who believe God. And He died for the world (Jn 1:29, 3:16, 4:42; 2 Cor 5:19; 1 Jn 2:2, 4:14) since all can come to and believe the One Who sent Christ. But Christ's shed blood will not atone for those who reject Christ. And if they reject Christ they do not belong to God. God justifies those that believe Him.

Irresistible Grace

There is no irresistible grace in the way that strict Calvinists teach. Nevertheless, no one will ever successfully resist the Holy Spirit when they truly believe God; hence they will come to Christ to be saved. The two faiths go together and cannot be broken. So if one says that they believe God yet they have no faith in Christ, they still do not truly believe God. He says that faith in Christ is a matter of life and death. Grace is irresistible to those who believe God for He gives Christ to them and them to Christ. This is the marriage made in heaven between Christ and the Church.

When we read the Scriptures in this way we arrive at a distinct way of understanding the concept of "irresistible grace." Our human choice is whether to believe God and to want to have a relationship with Him. If we choose to truly believe God we will do what He says which is to believe in Christ. He gives us to His Son for the new birth. By His Spirit we are born again.

But people can resist God, not believe Him and/or refuse to do what He says. And if they do so they will undoubtedly refuse to put their faith in Christ. True belief is always more than a mental consent to facts. Rather we must commit to Him, such that we will do His will which first, above all else, is to place our faith in His Son for salvation.

What is also clear from reading the texts in this way is that God decides whom He will give to Christ for the new birth. He decides who will be born again for such a birth is wrought by the will of God. Only God knows those that truly believe Him; He does a mighty transformation work in those that do (Eph 1:19). He gives us new life in Christ.

We must keep in mind that the Jewish writers begin with the faith of Abraham in the OT. In their Scriptures the promise of God is claimed by those who believe God. And Christ is the promised One, the One sent from God into this world. There is no salvation without faith in Christ.

From this "faith to faith" perspective neither strict Calvinists nor advocates of strict "free will" are quite correct in their dogma. They both leave out the need to believe God, the One Who sent the Son, in the first place. This would have been critical at the time of Christ and at the time when the epistles were first written. And this still holds true today for reasons already explained.

During the days of Christ and throughout the first years after the cross there was often a wide gap of time between believing God and faith in Christ. Would God have people make two decisions to believe Him? No, God is the One that gives us salvation, but only to those that believe Him. God does a powerful work in those that believe (Eph 1:18-20). He convinces us that His Son is the answer to our sin problem.

Perseverance of the Saints

If we have faith in Christ and His work on the cross, then God foreknew that we truly believed God. He then plants us, giving us the gift of salvation that comes by faith in Christ. All the texts that Calvinists use to show that what God starts He will complete are true. No one can take us out of God's hands or separate us from His love given to us in His Son.

As people whom God has redeemed in Christ, our destiny is secure. He has promised that we will live forever with Him. Once God grants us true salvation faith on the basis that we believe Him, God is faithful to work in us and through us to the end. We belong to Him and nothing can take us out of His hand or separate us from His love. We will gain the inheritance that He has promised. And in glory we will throw our crowns at the Lord's feet.

Summary of Faith to Faith

So does God choose us or do we choose God? God reveals Himself in many ways: through creation, Christ, the pages of the Word, His servants, and by the Holy Spirit. We choose to believe His witness to us, or not to believe. God knew those that would believe Him before the pre-dawn of creation and selected those that truly believe Him. These elect are predestined for faith in Christ, Who is God with us. They will be justified, conformed to the image of Christ, and in the end glorified.

The *ordo salutis* is "faith to faith," with set steps for us, but established by God before the dawn of the world. God does not cause people to believe, but He does predestine people to have faith in Christ when they truly believe what God has said. The new birth is spiritual and comes from God by His will. If we have the Spirit of God we will also have the Spirit of Christ (Rom 8:9). Absent the Spirit of Christ we still do not belong to God, as we still do not believe the One that sent His Son.

Chapter Nine

Does God Lie?

Let's now visit a few debates about doctrine that have been around for ages on end. Some have been heating up in recent years after being on the edge of extinction for a few decades. But before we go there, I want to make a few comments.

The main purpose for this book has been to show that there is an alternative to both the strict Calvin and Arminius views on the NT elect. Hence, both free will and God's choice for salvation warrant more study.

While the faith to faith approach may be true I have gone back and forth in my mind on whether to write this book lest it lead to a firestorm of controversy. We do not need more fights over doctrine. Rather we need to respect the views of others, live for Christ, and give thanks to God for what He has done.

There has been far too much acrimony between fellow Christians in the matter of "free will" in salvation. Lutzer (1998) was right when he wrote on this subject in his book: "The Doctrines that Divide." Whether we have the free will to believe in Christ has been a sore spot over the years for many theologians and Christians.

If the view offered in this book holds up under the scrutiny of Bible scholars from both camps then there should be little need to argue further over this point of doctrine. Both sides may be partly wrong and partly right. Perhaps God can take this book and help reduce some of the friction that permeates the two camps. This is my hope and prayer.

Truth can set us free from what divides. One day when we get to heaven we will know the full truth in this arena of doctrine, and then we will celebrate what God has said and done. We will have His full light on the Word that He has given us.

But we no doubt will continue to reap the wind of heated debate until Christ returns for His Church. I would wish this to be different, but that is the way we too often are in our old sin nature. And I suspect there will be those who will pull apart what has been written here as well. Pillars of human thought fossilized by years of claiming that "God has said" will not die easily.

While the "faith to faith" view explained in this book supports both camps in some ways, the proposed option also challenges a few of the basics held by most theologians in an epic, centuries' old debate. As you have no doubt seen by now I think that what is taught here fits with the texts of Scripture. Others will need to decide for themselves. If this exegesis endures the examination by those far more learned than I, then not a few commentaries will change along the way.

Both sides of the question on "free will" in salvation seem to miss a Scriptural sequence of believing the One Who sent the

Son to faith in the Son of God. This flow or repeated belief is spelled out most clearly in the Gospel of John, in his Epistles, and in Romans. As Paul said, *"The righteousness of God is revealed from faith to faith"* (Rom 1:17; cf 1 Jn 5:1-10 and Phil 3:9).

Bible scholars have failed to discern whom God's elect are (Rom 4:5; 4:24; 8:28-33). All seem to neglect and/or ignore those texts in the Word that deal with believing God, the One Who sent the Son, the One Who raised Him from the dead, and the One Who justifies. They undervalue those texts that say Abraham believed God, the One Who gave him the promise of One to come. They turn a deaf ear to Paul when he writes about believing the One Who raised Christ from the dead. And in Romans 4:24 Paul includes himself among those that believe God the Father.

Christ, Himself, did not ignore the need to believe the One Who sent Him (Jn 5:24). And Christ repeatedly stated that we need to believe that God sent Him. Believing God was bedrock to what He taught and in the accepted Scriptures of that day. And He claimed repeatedly that God the Father had turned all things over to Him. Still more, He said if the people knew God, they would believe Christ. What could be clearer? And would a spiritual birth occur absent believing the One who gives such a spiritual birth?

During Paul's day the NT was still to be written and compiled. When Paul sent a letter to a local church of that day the group of believers would only have that one letter plus the OT. However, what they received by courier would not have been seen as part of the Scriptures. This most certainly would have influenced how they would have read any of the first epistles that came their way.

Should we now circumvent believing God to have faith in the Son of God only? I do not think that Christ or the apostles ever taught this. Rather, I think Paul and John both wrote that if we are going to believe Christ, the One sent in the flesh, we must first truly believe the One that sent Him. As the disciple John wrote, *"If you love the Father you will also love the Son"* (1 Jn 5:1). This sounds like a sure thing to me, nearly the same thing that Paul said, but without the word predestine.

Through God's witness to us we come to faith in His Son, for His testimony is certain in those that believe Him (1 Jn 5:8-11). If we choose to believe and want to have a relationship with God, He has said to have faith in His Son; eternal life is in Him. Like Abraham we must still believe God Who gives us His promise, now fulfilled in His Son. We are to claim that promise by faith in Christ.

We must be careful not to think that anyone can come to Christ absent believing the One that sent Him. It won't happen and never has happened. They are One.

What Calvin savants have done in their doctrine, and this dates much earlier to "late" Augustine, is to ignore the need to believe the One Who sent the Son (Jn 5:24). In a sense they say we do not need to believe God. We only need to believe the second person of the Trinity, the One who is fully God and also fully Man. This indeed is a grievous omission. They teach "elect then faith." This is an absurd twist to the Scriptures! They never deal with the need to believe God the Father in the first place. And how do we know we are lost in sin, in need of a Savior if we do not believe God? And if we do not believe God, how would we ever recognize God with us, our Savior?

I doubt whether people in the pew, and most theologians, even realize that this is what high Calvinists teach. The unintentional deception is very subtle, but none the less real. No doubt most have given little thought to the implications of what they claim. And they have not seen or pursued the option suggested here.

The blind spot is further noted by their claim to believe God the Father in their creed; and I am certain that they do so. But they have failed to see the link in faith between God and Christ, the One sent. God the Father cannot have one set of believers and the Son of God another. But faith in Christ is revealed by believing God and He reveals the Trinity to us either through the Father or through the Son.

On the opposing side, those of Arminius, or strict "free will," persuasion have the same blind spot. Further trouble! Their elect are those that have faith in Christ. They teach "faith then elect." They too omit the need to believe the One Who promised, the One Who sent, the One Who raised Christ from the dead, the One Who sends His servants, the One whom we have not seen, the One Who now calls us, the One that requires the perfect sacrifice, the One Who justifies us when we place our faith in Jesus. Hence, they never quite grasp what Paul meant by predestination in Romans or Ephesians.

The word "predestine" for those who adhere to a strict "free will" view of salvation leads to problems in their doctrine. The word implies causation in some sense. And if God causes, then how is total free choice preserved? We are not free to put our faith in Christ without first truly believing God, what He has said about His Son, and what He has said about our sin and our need for a Savior to be adopted by Him.

Neither side in the debate has seen why the "faith to faith" concept was so critical in the historical era of Christ and Paul, and still is yet today. God has only one flock of sheep. We must believe both the One Who sent and the One sent. God does not justify anyone in Christ that does not truly believe God. In fact He will hide the identity of Christ from those who claim they know God but in reality not believe Him. Rather the new birth is given to those who truly believe the One Who sent Christ and raised Him from the dead. God grants grace and mercy to those who believe Him; we are born again with faith in Christ. God fulfills His promise to those who truly believe. He saves them by the power of His Word and Spirit.

I do not intend to make light of either side of the debate since they both omit the same thing. And I have gone back and forth between the two camps often thinking that something was not quite right. People from both sides are saved; all the justified believe God and put their faith in Christ. But the Scriptural exegesis by scholars from both sides has been muddled over the years because they misidentify God's elect.

God knows if and when we believe Him, and He knew this before the dawn of creation's first day. Yes, He knows us intimately and He predestined us to accept His Son, the One Who came in the flesh. God chose all that believe Him to have faith in His Son, to be adopted through Him. And now we are the children of God (Jn 1:12), fully righteous in His eyes.

The Son has always been part of the Godhead from the eternal past. His entrance into the world by virgin birth was planned before creation's first day, God knowing that Man would fall. But Christ came in the flesh at a point in time. Faith in Him, as we know today, was hidden (Gal 3:22-23; Eph 3:9-10; Rom 16:25; Mt 13:35) until He appeared at the apex of history past to shed His blood on our behalf.

And as the Greeks from a land beyond Palestine began to search for Christ just before His death, He then announced that He would draw all people to Himself (Jn 12:32). The world would soon know Who He was, if they would but heed the risen Lord. And without doubt the risen Lord is the foremost evidence of all ages that what God has said is true. Because of the cross and the empty tomb we have the sure evidence that God is Who He claims to be, and we also see that His Son is Who He claimed to be. And God, whether the Father or the Son, loves us.

The pivotal distinction between the view explained here and those endorsed by both strict Arminius and Calvin scholars is the need to believe God before we will see or grasp the need to put our faith in Christ. The premise is "faith to faith" (Rom 1:17). The elect are those who truly believe God, the One Who justifies (Rom 4:5; 8:33). They are certain to put their faith in Christ when God calls them to do so (Rom 8:28-30).

Is this not what would be taught to people at the time when the only Scriptures they had was the OT? Abraham was their role model and he believed God and claimed God's promise of One to come. Further, all authors of the NT were Jews, save one; believing God is their basis for all that happens. From that base He can choose anyone for His purpose. The Word says some are vessels for honorable use and some are vessels of wrath (Rom 9:21-22). God divides the vessels into those that believe Him and those that do not and He grants mercy and grace in Christ to those that do. And He chose to do this before the earth was formed.

In the OT God's purpose for the believer, whom God knew before their birth was two-fold. They were to claim the promise of the One to come for salvation and by faith serve the living God. Likewise in the NT God's purpose for those who believe Him is also two-fold. We are to put our faith in Christ for salvation, the promise now fulfilled; and also by faith serve Christ in His Church.

Now we might ask the question, "Does God choose people to believe Him?" There is no credible evidence in the Word that God does so. And we are not born again by trusting God, rather we are saved by faith in Christ, the second person of the Trinity (1 Jn 5:1-10), the One Who came in the flesh to die for us. And He was raised again.

God is sovereign in salvation; even believing God is not enough. But we will never arrive at a spiritual birth unless we believe Him. He welcomes all that will answer His call and believe His message about Christ. God has wonderful news for those who will believe Him.

If we omit or ignore all the texts which John and Paul wrote that speak about believing the One Who sent Christ, the One Who raised Him from the dead, the One Who justifies, we then have strict Calvinism.

Their view is that God chose His children with no condition whatsoever; we do not need to believe God nor the Son of God. God causes people to have faith in Christ, even though they do not even know that they need Him. This contradicts what the Word of God says. They violate one of the most basic and core axioms of all the Scriptures. We must truly believe God and claim His promise of the One to be sent, just as Abraham did. The Jewish authors of the NT had this right.

Pelagianism

I know that there will be those who accuse me of Pelagianism, or semi-Pelagianism. I am less concerned about labels and more concerned about what the Scriptures teach. And if you search the Scriptures you will find that what I have said is true.

What has been said here does not fit under the tent of Pelagianism, that Man can by means of works or self-effort achieve salvation. God indeed does the work of the new birth and regeneration. He has also done the work of revealing His plan to us through His Word.

He exercises great power through His Word toward us who believe (Eph 1:19). He gives us faith in Christ, our salvation, which will culminate in glorification. He indeed justifies us. Salvation is all through faith so that Man cannot boast that He has gained salvation by works (Eph 2:8-9). We would never come to faith in Christ unless God guided us with His Spirit using His Word in those who believe Him.

God desires to be merciful and gracious to all and He welcomes the "good" and the "evil" alike (Mt 22:10). We all come exactly the same way; we must answer His call to believe in Christ. He favors no person above another. He calls the weak and the strong, the great and the lowly, all in the same way. He is willing to give salvation to anyone that will believe the foolishness of the message preached, and this message is from God (1 Cor 1:21-2:1). Christ is God's wisdom for eternal life.

Flawed Doctrine and Voluntarist Thought

Does God lie? We have now come to the second reason why I have written this book. I have grown quite wearied by how some theologians see and represent God. I am fearful that many honorable Christian scholars advance a grotesque view of God. They respect, praise, and honor His power and authority; while they twist His love, His justice, and the way He uses His power.

God needs no defense, as He will do what He does regardless of what we think or teach for doctrine. Yet since the Scriptures tell us that we are to believe God, the One that sent His Son, then we best be as clear as we can be about Who He is and what He is like. The Word speaks for itself. But we must be careful how we handle Scriptural truth.

If we create a fantasy god in our minds, or distort what the Word says about God, then we may become like those who have a religious zeal for God, but still not know Him (Rom 10:1-4). Heaven forbid that we should misrepresent God to the world, to those who need to be saved, or to those who want to learn more about Him. God has charged us with the message of reconciliation (1 Cor 5:18). Let's not distort Who He is or what He says.

There is an infectious and contagious voice once again growing in the academic halls of Christendom. This voice faded for quite a few years; but once again the frothing din grows out of the strength of human logic. This voice impugns God's character and maligns His righteous ways. We are in for some dark days in the future should this perverse babble skew the minds of those that seek training in the Word.

There are those who teach that God causes people to reject God. Some go so far as to say that God caused the rebellion of Satan and the Fall of Man. This is the logical end, but a ruinous end, that comes from splitting God's sovereign rule from His unchanging character. Such thoughts twist and pervert the ways of God. Nothing in Scripture says this.

Some of these same professed theologians go further. They say that God plotted to have us become totally depraved in our sinful condition. And the reason God did this is so that His Son could be lifted up and receive glory and honor, to sum up all things in Christ (Eph 1:10). If you follow their logic, they claim God causes us to sin and then He gains glory for rescuing us from sin. What kind of a god is this?

They say that God wills to happen whatever He wants. His attributes and nature do not necessarily play any vital role in what He decrees or causes to happen. Since He is God He does not even need to adhere to the limits of His righteous ways. In other words He can act in contrary patterns. Above all else He is the God Who reigns. He doesn't even need to keep His promises. He can cause us to sin and/or not sin, simply because He wills it.

They claim that all the while God remains just because He acts in accordance with His will. Yet Man is still culpable and God is right for condemning people to Hell, even though they say that He was the One that caused the Fall of Man in the first place. No doubt a god could be like that, but he is not the One we see in Scripture.

If we live in a world where God reigns in the way they describe we indeed are the pawns in a fatalistic life and death deceitful scheme; we have naught to say about our final end.

Our fate was sealed before we took our first breath. If our destiny happens to be heaven, then that is certainly nice and we can rejoice, but what about the people who are bound for a lost eternity. But more than this, what does this say about God and His Word?

To the honor of God's name, the Word does not teach that God's rule lies beyond His immutable nature. God reigns in perfect harmony with His nature and the virtues of his character. His will comes forth from the purity and Holiness of His truth that never changes, for His Word is truth; and He expresses His will through His Word. There is no variation or shifting shadow with God, and every good and perfect gift is from Him (James 1:17).

The will of God cannot be above truth, for He is truth. His virtues shape what righteousness is all about. To divorce His ruling power from the perfections of His character will destroy what the Word says about God and His promises.

Those who say that God causes all actions of every person sabotage His message of love for all. A god who causes people to reject him cannot be just for sending people to hell. Such thought is anathema. Those who go a step further and say that God even causes Satan to do what He does have rendered the death of truth; they ascribe evil to God. The logic of such does not befit those who teach of God. Be careful of those who tweak off a mite from the web of evil and call it good; God does not change.

Christ revealed what God is like and He was full of grace and truth (Jn 1:14). For this book I emphasize **truth**. But that is not what is being said by those who sift the Word through the filter of their human inspired reasoning.

The Rise of Voluntarist Thought

Most of this abject human logic is no recent marvel to the church at large. Radical Voluntarists have been around a long time. I will not pursue all the ins and outs of the development of thought in this arena, but here are some of the twists that have taken place over the years.

The first to wander part way down this dark road was "late" Augustine in the 400's. He never quite went as far as those who would come later since he taught that Man had the free choice to sin or not sin before the Fall. But in his later years he held that Man could only sin after the Fall due to our depraved nature. To do anything but sin God must step in with mercy and grace. And according to his view even faith in Christ is not possible without God's grace.

While we do indeed need God's grace, and even permission, to come to faith in the Son, Augustine ignored the need to believe the One Who sent the Son before saving faith in Christ. And ever since that time many have followed in his footsteps and the path has spiraled downward.

Problems come from Augustine's teaching. "Why does God save some?" And if He is the One who chooses arbitrarily before we believe in Christ, then where is God's love for all people? Why does He not give all a chance? And if He chooses to save some He must also then pass by others and let them go to Hell. And if He loves only some, what does this say for His justice?

Of course the argument comes that God owes no one salvation, which is clearly true from the Scriptures. Yet the teaching seems to undermine God's love for all (Jn 3:16). And the Scriptures leave no doubt that God desires all to be saved (1 Tm 2:4; 2 Pt 3:9; Ezek 18:23, 33:11). Does God lie?

The darkness deepened in later years after Augustine, and the path got more serpentine on down the path of time and theological study. Some scholars began to argue that if we can only do things that come from our nature then how could those who were of a perfect nature in Eden stoop to sin? Adam and Eve were created with no sin nature. Hence, something must have made them sin and the same thing must have caused Satan to revolt, as he was also created perfect. What made them do so?

Then they read in the Scriptures that God chose us in Christ before He hung the world in space (Eph 1:4). And they find that God has a grand purpose to sum up all things in Christ (Eph 1:10). Hence, God must have had the revolt of Satan and the Fall of Man planned all along. And He is sovereign; He could have created Man so that he would not have sinned.

These same scholars search the Word and find how God allowed Satan to do what he did to Job (Job 1:8-12; 2:3-6). And God sent an evil spirit to Saul (1 Sam 18:10), or hardened Pharaoh's heart (Ex 10:1), or arranged sin to happen in certain ways (Gn 37:18-36; 45:7-8). And God sent a lying spirit (1 Kgs 22:20-22) to defeat an army, and God will do so again in the last days (2 Thes 2:11). And since God has and will do these things He must cause all of what evil and human forces do.

They conclude from selected Scriptures that God causes sin, and that earlier He orchestrated the demise of Satan and the Fall of Man. To them God has a secret design, hidden from Man but known to Himself. He is behind the scenes causing evil, so that in the end He can exalt Christ and bring glory to Him. And if one follows the logic then many are victims so that God can gain accolades from those He saves. He causes Man to sin so that He can gain glory for rescuing Man. All this is fatalistic. A breath taking "Oh my," do we worship a God like that? Does God lie?

Some of the first Reformers in the 16th century were held captive to Voluntarist thought. We dare not devalue the work or teaching of these men as they are giants of the faith and we owe them (Luther, Calvin, and Zwingli) an immense debt of gratitude. Some agreed that God chose people to be saved, to give them faith in Christ. They saw that this is all of God's grace. And they thought God's choice was arbitrary, based on nothing except His sovereign will to choose whosoever He would. Most of them were heavily influenced by Augustine.

But the question remains, "Whom does God choose for salvation?" Does God's Word say anything about this? Further, what did Christ say?

Moreover, some scholars also thought that those not so chosen were reprobate and on their way to hell, doomed before they were ever born. And if they held that God also caused the Fall, then God rules and causes all decisions we will ever make. And this they say is so even though it seems to us that we make the choices. To them we do nothing more, nor nothing less than what God intends for us to do. Yet God holds us accountable for the sin that He causes while He says that we do it. Does God lie?

Since the days of reform, theologians have gone back and forth on these issues with no end in sight. Some of the great missionaries and evangelists of the past 300 years have held some of these views. Most have not. Rather they are more apt to hold a "free will" bent while knowing that God rules over all things. During most of the 1900's there was little friction between the two camps. Each tolerated the other's views and more or less kept to themselves.

But in the last two decades, the heat has started to rise once again. Both camps, each certain that they are right, have become more assertive as they try to persuade the other of the supposed "error of their way." Sadly, both could be wrong in certain respects. But such marks the story of theology.

For the most part the debate takes place on the academic stage of study in theology; but the issues have started to spill over to local churches. Those who warm the pews by and large do not have enough Bible acumen to assess what is being taught in this arena; yet many sense that things are not quite right.

Part of the problem is that most moderate and strict "free will" proponents are not able to hold their own with those of an extreme Calvin view when it comes to the exegesis of the Word. Hence, many that love the Word are charmed and taken in by this thinking.

Those new to such study are seldom aware of the extreme slant in thought that leads to the conclusion that God causes sin; a required end if we claim that God controls all decisions that we will ever make. And as they browse the selected texts most fail to see that certain Scriptures are taught while others are left untouched. Problems then develop.

I doubt that most teachers of Voluntarist thought even realize this. I have read many books and articles from a strict Calvin point of view and have yet to see any of them take seriously those texts that deal with believing the One Who sent Christ. And they say nothing about believing the One Who raised Him from the dead. Hence their logic leads to double predestination. If God does not choose you then you are destined to Hell. If God does choose you then you will be in heaven.

The question is whether God's choice is arbitrary. The Scriptures do not say that His choice is arbitrary. He chooses those that believe Him. In the OT God reckoned them as righteous and in the NT God gives them the righteousness of His Son, all through faith.

By picking certain texts that point to God causing all things they say that God has a secret will. He not only allows and uses evil for His purposes, which is no problem for any view; but they say He causes evil too, albeit through secondary sources that He incites. Some skillful teachers do not state this up front. Rather they let those taught draw their own conclusions. But the end is fixed by the human logic that guides the thought. Their thinking is fatalistic.

Let me list a few things that result from this ultra-deterministic logic. This is not exhaustive; rather only a taste is needed.

1. God is just for sending people to Hell even though He was the One that caused them to sin.

2. God speaks and then He also causes Satan to ask, "Hath God said?"

3. Satan is a liar but God causes Him to lie.

4. The Holy Spirit convicts of sin while at the same time God causes us to sin.

5. God causes us to love God, hence God loves Himself.

6. God can promise but He can also break a promise if He so wishes.

7. Christ was not really full of grace and truth.

8. God really caused all the "I wills" of Satan.

9. God is merciful to what He causes to happen—He is merciful to Himself yet punishes people for what He causes them to do.

10. When God sent His prophets He really intended for people to resist the prophets and rebel.

11. God really wanted some people to turn to idols and not worship Him.

12. God desires that some go to Hell so that He can gain more glory.

13. God lied when He said He loved the world

14. God actually lied when He said in His Word that He wants all to be saved.

Satan takes great sport with this kind of contorted reasoning. He tried to get Job to accuse God of evil and curse Him. After all if we are mere pawns in God's life and death game plan then He did not really create us in freedom or in love. In fact He did not create a person, rather a humanoid. Nor is God, in fact, just. If I had to describe this extreme view, it sounds like they think God is more evil than Satan. But I must say that there are some Christian scholars on the fringe who hold to these things, and some are very skilled in the Word.

I doubt that most from the sovereign side of the debate would care to think of God in this way. But they are certainly going to emphasize God's will over God's love when it comes to salvation.

Their thoughts about the justice of God do not add up. That God would hold Man accountable for what He causes to happen is beyond reason. Now a god could do that, but is that the One that we see in the Word. Is that the One Who loved the world so much that He sent His Son to die for us on the cross?

I think not, and I do not find the Scriptures that teach this. Hence there must be a way that God predestines some to be saved, while still being just for hiding Who Christ is from others and sending them to Hell. There must be a way to read the Scriptures so that we can believe the message of God's love. Love is not needed if all is determined.

There must be a way that God does not act in conflicting ways. There must have been a reason to send His prophets who spoke for Him, and His servants that wrote the Word, then hide the message from some but give it to others. We must believe God and only then can we understand what He says. God hides the meaning of what He has said to those that do not truly believe Him. They never learn anything from God though they may think they do so.

Logic Guided by Scripture

Scholars on all sides of the question about "free will" have not seen the sequence of believing God to faith in Christ. I have found only two that have touched on the "faith to faith" (Rom 1:16-17) phrase written by Paul. Neither of them saw the significance.

No commentary that I have read sees the "elect" in the way set forth in this book. Those skilled in the Word give short shrift to the phrase "faith to faith" in spite of the context, the prime manifesto of what is to come later in the book of Romans. As we have seen Paul warned of repeated faith three times through the space of two verses in his proviso to his letter to the people of Rome.

I would encourage those skilled in the original Greek to take a second long look. Still more, the Greek word for "believe" in the NT most often refers to repeated or continuous action. Might this verb be in the text to guide us? Can we have a true grasp of soteriology without taking this into account?

Bible scholars do not deal with this verb form very well when it comes to salvation, nor with the phrase "faith to faith." Most simply ignore these things. Such language does not fit the template of the doctrinal creed of most. But that does not rule out that God is faithful to those that believe Him. Believing God is more important than having all the right answers.

All traditional "free will" views of which I am aware have identified God's elect as those with faith in Christ. But if "faith to faith" and believe are repeated actions, then the elect most likely are those that start by believing God, the One Who justifies (Rom 4:5), the same One that raised Christ from the dead (Rom 4:24). And the difficult passages of Romans eight and nine make much more sense if read as "faith to faith."

In a sense God brings His people, those that believe Him, into a "marriage" bond, with His Son, sealed by the Holy Spirit of promise. How does God the Father and Christ have the same flock of sheep without some such certainty? None the less, if a person never comes to faith in Christ they never believed God in the first place.

So God foreknows those that believe Him. He calls them and gives them salvation, that is "faith in Christ." For He has said if you believe Me and My Word, put your faith in My Son. The Holy Spirit is indeed irresistible to those who truly believe God. We are born again by the Spirit (Jn 3:5-6). God seems to unfold the Trinity to those that believe. We learn more and more what God is like.

Hence we do have a measure of free will. We can believe God and His Word or we can choose not to believe God and His Word. God foreknew those of us that would, and He predestines (causes) us to be born again in Christ. He hands all that belong to Him over to His Son. No one that truly believes God will fail to put their faith in Christ if they want a relationship with God.

The beauty of seeing the Scriptures in this way, other than being the truth, is that now the logic of radical Voluntarism no longer traps us. We are not compelled to think in terms of fatalism or strict determinism. God foreknows something which He does not appear to cause. The choice may only be one, but it only takes one. Just as in the Garden of Eden there was one choice, so now there is one choice. Do we choose to believe God or not to believe Him?

People are accountable for rejecting God. God is then just when He does not allow them to come to faith in Christ for they do not believe God. And God is more than just for sending people to Hell; they refuse to heed His call to come to His Son.

Knowing and Causing

Scholars absorbed by strict Calvin convictions hold that God rules in all things. As always we must define what this means to them. They think that God causes all actions of people, both sin and righteous acts. They derive this idea from the texts that say some are predestined by God to be justified and glorified. But they see no precondition, except God's arbitrary choice, for one to be saved by faith in Christ. And if God chooses to save, He, by omission, chooses for Hell. So the offer from God is only for those whom God chose to save before the earth was formed.

The hub of the entire dispute rests in whether Man can make his own choice to some degree. This is why the "elect" of the NT is such a crucial group of people in this dispute of religio-philosophical thought. Man must have a measure of free will for God to be just and hold us responsible for sin. To say that God determines all actions, no matter if through primary or secondary causes, renders null and void God's just action in judgment. And such teaching rips the heart out of the message of God's love for all people.

The religio-philosophical bias posed by such scholars states that since God knows He causes. They claim that in order for God to know with certainty He must control the action of all people at all times. Without such control He could not know the future. And the future is certain for those prophesied events that are yet to come.

There is no Scriptural or logical reason to limit what God can know to what He causes. That is human inspired reasoning. If God were bound by time then this of course would be inevitable, but God knows the beginning from the end all at the same time. Hence God rules over the actions of people by knowing all the details of what takes place. And of course He intervenes to bring to pass what He has said will take place so that His Word is true. There is no doubt that He controls far more than most think. He always sets limits to what He allows.

Still, we must make a distinction between knowing what He
permits and causing what He wants to happen.

Some from a moderate Calvin position try to deal with these
issues when they propose the idea that God determines through
Man's free will. This is Geisler's (2001) approach. God
predetermines at the same time He knows. There is no
precondition for faith in Christ. There is no sequence in logic or
in time between God knowing and God causing. Then Geisler
caves in and says we don't know how this works, the mystery is
too great for us to fathom (summary of his first chapter).

He, in essence, admits that he has not solved the Scriptural
problem, yet he knows that both must somehow be true. And I
say "Amen," to that, both free will and God causing must be
true. But in the end Geisler's reasoning from the Scriptures
comes up on the weak side, short of an adequate explanation.

I think what has been explained in this book conforms to the
texts. And what I have written reveals a serious problem. The
views about the elect of God for both Calvin and Arminius
scholars may not quite line up with the texts of Scripture.

We must keep distinct what God foreknows from what He
causes in order to confirm that man has free will. The problem is
solved here if the causal sequence (though not always a time
sequence) is "faith to faith." God foreknows those that believe
Him and He predestines them to faith in Christ. He chooses all
those that have faith in Him to have faith in Christ. God's elect
are those with true faith in God, the One that justifies (Rom 4:5;
8:33) the One that raised Christ from the dead (Rom 4:24). Faith
in Christ, our salvation, comes by a spiritual birth given to those
that indeed believe God. We will not recognize any need for a
Savior if we do not believe God first. And can we believe God
with us, Immanuel, if we do not believe the One that sent the
Son.

God knew us (we that truly believe God) from the beginning and He has predestined us to be saved, to have faith in His Son. His purpose is to justify, glorify, and conform all who truly believe Him into the image of His Son. Just as Abraham believed God and claimed His promise, so we believe God and claim His promise, now fulfilled, by faith in Christ.

God knows all things, every action that we do, free and otherwise, from the past, present, and future. And He knows these things at all times, from the very beginning. In contrast what God causes is a more restricted set of actions. But these do not include all that God sees and knows. By His will acting on what He knows He maintain, rule over, and guide the affairs of men. He is never taken by surprise.

He also knows all contingencies. He knows that if He would allow people or evil forces to do what they want then things would happen that would prevent what He desires to come to pass. He permits no such things. Hence He seems to have many things that He only allows under prescribed circumstances, those that serve His purposes.

Then there are things that God directly rules. Believing God seems to be our choice, but faith in Christ is God's choice for us who believe Him. Hence faith in Christ, the second person of the Trinity (Who is God with us), is on the list of what God causes to happen. Faith in God and whether to believe His Word is our choice. And if we do we will not fail to put our faith in Christ for God has said to do so. He has determined that all who believe Him will have faith in Christ. His Word declares this. We are not saved by faith in God though we have passed from death to life; we are born again by faith in Christ and He is our righteousness before God. God justifies those that believe. He hands us over to His Son as Scripture states very clearly.

From the evidence written in the texts of Scripture, "free will" lives. God's love for all in the world is genuine. God's justice is upheld. We see God's power through His Word and by

His Spirit as they bring forth salvation, faith in Christ, to the souls who believe God. Indeed this birth is spiritual wrought by God in those that have learned from Him. He foreknew us by our faith in Him. And now we have faith in Christ, the One sent; and through the Son, we have faith in God. The proof of our faith in God is our faith in Christ.

Whosoever will may come. And if we believe God, He will plant us in His Son. He adopts us by faith in Christ, for the righteousness of Christ, that which is perfect, becomes our righteousness. His work on the cross paid the penalty of death for our sin. And what God plants and will be secure for all eternity. No one can take us out of God's hands. We are sealed by the Holy Spirit of promise. And in the end we will worship Him in glory.

So Abraham believed God and claimed His promise. And now we believe God and claim the promise of God fulfilled in Christ. All that truly believe God will be saved, none will be left out as they are all given to the Son; for salvation is in Him. Who can bring a charge against God's elect for God is the One Who justifies. And He justifies those that have faith in Him. What a wonderful God and Savior we have. God does not lie. He is full of grace and truth.

Bibliography

Alford, H. *Ephesians, in The Greek Testament. Vol. 3*, Chicago, IL, Moody Press, 1958.

Barth, K. *Church Dogmatics, Volume II—The Doctrine of God, Part 2.* trans. by Bromiley, G. W., Torrence, T. F. (ed.), Edinburgh: T. and T. Clark, 1967.

Demarest, B. *The Cross and Salvation: The Doctrine of Salvation* (J. Feinberg, ed.) Wheaton, IL, Crossway Books, 1997.

Edwards, J., A Divine and Supernatural Light, Immediately Imparted to the Soul by the Spirit of God, Shown to be Both a Scriptural and Rational Doctrine, (1734) in *The Works of Jonathan Edwards*, (2nd ed.), Hickman, E., Edinburgh: Banner of Truth Trust, 1974.

Geisler, N. L. *Chosen but Free* (2nd ed.) Minneapolis, MN, Bethany House Publishers 2001.

Hanson, C. Young, Restless, Reformed. *Christianity Today*, September, 2006.

Hunt, D. & White, J. *Debating Calvinism.* Sisters, OR, Multnomah Publishers, 2004.

Luther, Martin. *Bondage of the Will, (1525)* trans. by Packer, J. I., and Johnston, O. R., Grand Rapids, MI, Baker Publications, 1990.

Lutzer, E. W. *The Doctrines that Divide: A Fresh look at the Historic Doctrines that Separate Christians.* Grand Rapids, MI, Kregel Publications, 1998.

Olson, C. *Beyond Calvinism and Arminianism.* Cedar Knolls, NJ, Global Gospel Ministries, 2002.

Picirilli, R. *Grace Faith Free Will.* Nashville, TN, Randall House, 2002.

Pink, A. W., *The Sovereignty of God.* Grand Rapids, MI, Baker Book House, 1984.

Pinnock, C., Rice, R., Sanders, J., Hasker, W., Basinger, D. *The Openness of God.* Downers Grove, IL, Inter Varsity Press, 1994

Piper, J. *The Pleasures of God.* Sisters, OR: Multnomah Publishers, 2000.

Piper, J., *The Justification of God.* (2nd ed), Grand Rapids, MI, Baker Academic, 1993.

Schreiner, T. & Ware, B. (ed.) *Still Sovereign: Contemporary Perspectives on Election, Foreknowledge, and Grace.* Grand Rapids, MI, Baker Books, 2000.

Shank, R. *Life in the Son.* Minneapolis, MN, Bethany House Publishers, 1989

Sproul, R. C. *Chosen by God.* Wheaton, IL, Tyndale House, 1986.

Tenny, M. C. New Testament Times. Grand Rapids, MI, Baker Book House, 2004.

Vance, L. M. The Other Side of Calvinism. Pensacola, FL, Vance Publications, 1999.

White, J. R., The Potter's Freedom. Amityville, NY, Calvary Press, 2000.

White, J. R. The God Who Justifies. Minneapolis, MN, Bethany House, 2001.

Subject Index

Scripture Index

Printed in the United States
79133LV00003B/1-114